Spiritual
Intelligence

Spiritual
Intelligence

Discover Your SQ.
Deepen Your Faith.

ALAN E. NELSON

BakerBooks

a division of Baker Publishing Group
Grand Rapids, Michigan

© 2010 by Alan E. Nelson

Published by Baker Books
a division of Baker Publishing Group
P.O. Box 6287, Grand Rapids, MI 49516-6287
www.bakerbooks.com

Printed in the United States of America

Library of Congress Cataloging-in-Publication Data
Nelson, Alan E.
    Spiritual intelligence : discover your SQ. deepen your faith / Alan E. Nelson.
        p.   cm.
    ISBN 978-0-8010-7193-5 (pbk.)
    1. Spiritual formation. I. Title.
BV4511.N45 2009
248.4—dc22   2009033622

10   11   12   13   14   15   16   7   6   5   4   3   2   1

In keeping with biblical principles of creation stewardship, Baker Publishing Group advocates the responsible use of our natural resources. As a member of the Green Press Initiative, our company uses recycled paper when possible. The text paper of this book is comprised of 30% postconsumer waste.

green
press
INITIATIVE

Contents

Acknowledgments

I'd like to thank some friends and mentors:

Ray and Anne Ortlund, who saw some potential in a young couple like Nancy and myself and invested time as our Path Finders.

Thom and Joani Schultz, whom God has used amazingly to transform people around the world with their creative ideas and infective passion.

And Chad Allen, an incredible editor who saw the worth in this project. While Formica countertops are functional, I prefer granite. Thanks for the upgrades, Chad.

My soul mate, Nancy, who has been Jesus in my midst more times than I can imagine. Forgive my moments of blindness.

Foreword

As a university professor I've often fantasized about a pill I could offer my students each semester to boost their intelligence. On the first day of class, I'd say something like, "After we read through the syllabus, I'd like you to each take one of these little pills I'm handing out, and we will reconvene tomorrow." They'd file into the classroom the next day, each with a higher IQ than the day before. Wouldn't it be marvelous? In my dream, the semester is filled with lively discussions and intelligent questions. I see students learning not only from me, but from each other as they bring in outside reading that wasn't even assigned. I see them digging through the library for more and more knowledge. As one insight is gleaned, it feeds the curiosity and desire for finding another. My students are passionate about learning—not to get a grade, but for the pure enjoyment of improving their minds. They wake up each morning eager to get to class. And their excitement for learning propels me to teach like never before as we share the journey of increasing our intelligence. By semester's end, I have grown a small army of intellectual giants. Can you imagine? I suppose it's every teacher's dream.

I've also had a similar secret wish about the church. Every year, I'm privileged to preach to some of the finest congregations in North America. And on countless occasions, I've shared Sunday brunch with a minister and asked, "Well, do you think I got through?" He knows exactly what I'm asking: *Did my message make a difference?* The typical response is positive and affirming—what else are you going to say to a guest in your pulpit? But I have a hunch he wonders the same thing I do as I climb onto an airplane and head back home. Did the souls of the people in the pews grow? Or was it just another routine Sunday of suiting up and going through the motions? And the more I meet with ministers, the more I'm convinced that they, in week after week of ministering to their parishioners, are wondering the same thing.

That's why I am so very excited about the book you hold in your hands. Alan Nelson has given us a tremendous tool for growing our souls. Alan has succinctly noted the ways and means for improving our spiritual understanding. And he is the first to admit that his insights are not uniquely his own; they rest on the principles Jesus taught two thousand years ago.

In *Spiritual Intelligence*, Alan has delineated the activities, insights, and skills of the people who have a higher "spiritual quotient," and how it is they bring about this growth. He has studied their moves and reveals them to us in this volume. He shows us that these people are not the spiritual elite; they are individuals like you and me who have learned to expand their capacity for God and have become more confident and competent in his ways.

If you are yearning to grow your soul as well as the souls of others; if you want to ratchet up your spiritual know-how, get ready to be challenged on one page and inspired on another. *Spiritual Intelligence* is the best book I've read in years for helping people cultivate a deep and authentic spirituality. This book has the potential to awaken the all-too-dormant life that lies within the soul of far too many churches. And every person who is serious about improving his or her SQ should read and reread its pages.

Spiritual Intelligence is not a fantasy pill to swallow—it won't give you "three easy steps to spiritual wholeness"—but it affords articulate and meaningful answers to soul-searching questions, as well as proven practices that are sure to lead you into a deeper relationship with Jesus—an intelligent relationship that will impact who you are, what you do, and how you do it.

Les Parrott III, PhD,
Seattle Pacific University,
Author of *Becoming Soul Mates*

Introduction

From Pampers to Depends

If you're like most people, you believe you have a soul. Nearly everyone these days is interested in soul growth to some degree. Whether it's the popularity of Osteen, Ortberg, or Oprah, our culture has demonstrated an appetite for faith and spirituality. Chances are you possess at least a modest desire to develop spiritually. You may or may not have found organized religious or church events helpful. Whether you have is not necessarily pertinent to this book, but it may be to understanding why I've written it. You see, a growing number of pastors, researchers, and authors like myself have become disappointed with the results we've seen in people after years of church involvement.

The reason is not, as some might believe, too many liberal, gospel-lite preachers. Nor is it a sheer lack of motivation among those pursuing faith. Most of my observations come from the entrails of committed evangelicalism. I was reared in a very conservative Baptist church, followed by Pentecostal influence, and then I pastored congregations in the holiness movement for over twenty years. All of these are traditions that pride themselves in applying orthodox Christianity.

In all my observations, one question has plagued me more than the rest. In spite of decades of worship services, Bible studies, ministry involvement, building campaigns, revival services, and church board meetings, why do so many Christians seem so petty, negative, cantankerous, easily offended, judgmental, critical, and grace deficient? Certainly we would think they'd be different from those "outside" the church. I have witnessed far too many church attendees behaving badly, and numerous other leaders testify to the same observations. How can so many years of involvement in faith events and programs yield such pitiful results? To be honest, this is a personal question as much as anything else. I too have had an up-and-down life of faith in spite of being raised in the church and immersed in Bible studies, prayer meetings, small groups, and professional training.

There has to be a better way to catalyze spiritual growth and significantly improve the return on our investment of religious activities and church programs. Think of the satisfaction of seeing your own life change, becoming the person you dreamed of, and having others affirm your growth. Consider the fun of journeying with a group, helping each other develop—like a *Friends* series with soul. I'm convinced that if we investigate the methods of how Jesus interacted with his key followers, we will find the secret of that success; how in three short years, he molded soulish lumps of clay into spiritually mature people who would forever change the world with his message.

Growing Up in Church

Like many American midwesterners, I grew up in church, almost literally. First Baptist in downtown Creston, Iowa, was a brick and spire building with stained-glass windows and a pipe organ—the works. Theater seating and padded pews hadn't evolved for churches yet, so on the rare occasion that I was allowed to fall asleep during a service, I leaned on my mom's shoulder or we doubled up Dad's suit jacket as a pew pillow. Little girls' bare legs squeaked when they scooted up or back on the hard oak benches.

One muggy Sunday evening in 1964, Pastor Crown's sermon on hell, combined with the non-air-conditioned humidity of rural Iowa, convinced my five-year-old mind that I didn't want to spend eternity in Hades when I died. So at the end of the service, when we sang "Just As I Am" and the invitation was given for people to come forward to accept Jesus, I tugged at my mom's sleeve. She whispered to my dad, and he nodded. Down the aisle Mom and I walked. Afterward, Pastor Crown took me and my parents to the prayer room off to the left of the platform, where I prayed the sinner's prayer.

Every Sunday, we took a road trip, fifteen miles via country roads, to attend Sunday school and worship service. We would return home for lunch (which we called "dinner" on Sundays), feed the animals, and then drive back for evening youth group and worship service. On Wednesday, we'd return for prayer meeting followed by choir practice. There were additional revival meetings, potlucks, Easter and Christmas cantatas, and vacation Bible school. My dad wasn't a pastor, but he may as well have been. I grew up in church—enjoying most of it, enduring the rest.

So it should have been no surprise when I eventually studied for the ministry, served God as a youth pastor at a small church, worked as an associate pastor at a megachurch, and planted two congregations from scratch, moving them into their own buildings. I've now authored more than a dozen books on church leadership and spiritual growth, as well as hundreds of articles. And for a few years, I have served pastors and ministry leaders as the executive editor of a national magazine, not to mention teaching dozens of workshops and seminary courses, and networking with national church leaders. I've bored you with my resume because after half a century of attending church and two decades of pastoring and resourcing the shepherds, I've come to a frightful conclusion: few churches know how to take you where you need to go.

I haven't given up on church. I really like pastors. My heart goes out to them. They are, except for a few bad apples, some of the most wonderful and committed people on the planet who, unfortunately, are often overworked and underappreciated. I attend a local church where my ordained wife is on staff. I enjoy networking with pastors and church leaders across the country. And my prayer is that churches will find this book to be a vibrant resource for the spiritual growth of their members. (Appendix B in the back of this book is specifically for church leaders who want to implement the methods in this book among their congregations.)

But my frustration is with the limited Christlikeness in church attendees, those who seem to transition from Pampers to Depends, with little to no maturation in between. Many of my clergy colleagues confess that the return on investment isn't nearly what they'd like it to be. The temptation is to blame the people in the seats, suggesting that if only they were more dedicated and willing to sacrifice, they'd experience the transformation we preach. We point our fingers at a secular culture, the sin nature, inadequate funds, and lousy preaching. But I think there's a more strategic problem at work here.

"Oh, Grow Up"

So why do so many good, committed, veteran churchgoers become frustrated with their spiritual growth? Why are divorce rates in the church similar to those outside? If over 80 percent of Americans say they're Christian, and a fourth of over three hundred million U.S. citizens claim to be evangelicals, why does our society struggle so much with drug abuse, incarceration, violence, materialism, pornography, alcoholism, and numerous other social ills? Sociologists suggest that as few as 5 percent of a given population can change societal norms, and 16 percent constitutes a critical mass. Wouldn't you think that the 25 percent of the U.S. population who claim personal faith would make more of a difference in our cultural landscape? Why do long-term members gossip, leave their church over petty board arguments, and run their pastors out of town? What causes them to withhold their offerings when the preacher says something that irritates them, or quit a ministry because they don't get along with someone in it? Is sin so powerful that God can't significantly change us? Why isn't the gospel more transformational? Could we have missed something along the way?

I believe the answer is related to a concept I refer to as *spiritual intelligence* (SI). A few years ago, psychologist Daniel Goleman and his colleagues wrote a bestselling book called *Emotional Intelligence* (EI). While they did not originate the concept of EI, they popularized it. EI explains why some people are well-balanced, cultivate healthy relationships, and respond effectively to difficult circumstances while most people, on the other hand, are less stable, upset easily by others, and frustrate quickly when things don't go their way. The resiliency and relational health that emotional intelligence provides are powerful characteristics of people who live well. In a similar but more soulish fashion, spiritual intelligence is about a person's ability to assimilate faith—what he or she learns in Christian community, Bible study, worship, and prayer—into everyday life. In short, the fact that so few exhibit Jesus-like qualities despite decades of attending church is a matter of low SI.

The good news is that just as researchers suggest we can raise our EI quotient, most of us can improve our SI quotient as well. We do this not necessarily by finding a better church, listening to more pithy sermons, becoming more committed, tithing or serving more, or simply trying harder. The solution is not to mimic Jesus through self-control, like a weight lifter straining under a barbell. *The key is to understand and practice the methods that Jesus used with his disciples, so that we become like him and acquire true maturity.* This isn't a book about doing church differently. It's about you.

Jesus provides a path to spiritual intelligence. We can learn his methods as we look at biblical records of how he transformed the lives of nearly a dozen men in less than three years, who in turn revolutionized history. Christian living books, Bible studies, gospel iTunes, CDs, seminars, conferences, television and radio programs, ministry websites, and over three hundred thousand churches in the U.S. offer to help us develop. But unless these tools coincide with the methods of Jesus, we'll fall short of spiritual maturity. The solution is not so much the "what" as it is the "how." SI presents a pattern, a framework for developing your own soul growth plan, based on how Jesus developed his followers.

Section I

A Spiritual Journey

ONE

It's Your Soul

*Taking Responsibility
for Your Own Spiritual Growth*

Great news! You can grow your soul. If you're like an increasing segment in society, you're interested in developing the spiritual dimension of your life that in turn impacts every other area, such as attitudes, relationships, self-image, character, decision making, work, purpose, family, leisure, health, sex, and finances. People are looking for answers and that's exciting. Rick Warren's book on purpose sold over twenty-five million copies. Joel Osteen's books on a better life became *New York Times* bestsellers. Oprah ran a webinar on spirituality that attracted more than two million people and temporarily overloaded their system. People are motivated to discover what it takes to get to the next level spiritually.

So what is it that makes a person soul smart? While I'm not an expert on world religions, I have investigated the life of Jesus and worked for years on the principles you have in your hand, and I'm convinced you can apply the same methods Jesus used to grow the souls of his followers. What may surprise you is how different it is from how most pursue their spirituality.

What's Your Spirituality Quotient (SQ)?

As IQ is to intelligence, SQ is to spirituality. A significant disconnect exists between what most people profess to believe and how they live on a daily basis. This gap between passive and active faith disillusions people who observe professing followers of Jesus and see little difference in how they live. Far too often, church attendance falls short in stimulating life change. Why, after so many years of hearing sermons, singing praise songs, studying the Bible, and serving, do so few reflect the qualities we read about in Jesus and expect from his followers?

Spiritual intelligence is the process leading to maturity, based on the methods of Jesus. The concept transcends the pop slogan "WWJD?" (What would Jesus do?). Four-step discipleship plans, forty-day campaigns, and sequential curriculum programs can be practical tools, but a more fundamental and flexible methodology is needed that results in a personalized, lifelong approach to growth.

People with spiritual intelligence, or a high SQ, aren't Mother Teresa clones. They are every bit themselves with unique personalities, backgrounds, pet peeves, gifts, looks, and tastes. But they exude an array of attractive characteristics, including:

- Love, joy, peace, patience, gentleness, faith, goodness, and self-control, in and out of stressful situations (Gal. 4:22–23)
- Modeling spiritual teaching (Heb. 6:1–2)
- Strong faith (Matt. 17:20)
- A lifestyle consistent with faith (James 2:14–26)
- Confession of spiritual failure (Ps. 51)
- Humility in attitude and service (Phil. 2:3–11)

Who wouldn't want these qualities in their spouse, boss, employees, children, friends, neighbors, or themselves?

Who's Responsible?

Who's looking out for your spiritual growth? Who do you depend on to strengthen your faith and connect you with your Creator? Many might think of their favorite author, speaker, or religious leader. But will Rick Warren, Joel Osteen, Robert Schuller, Beth Moore, Joyce Meyer, T. D. Jakes, Max Lucado, or the pope personally advise you? What about your local priest or pastor? If you're one of a growing percentage of people attending a megachurch, there's little chance you'll have quality, individual time with the lead pastor. I know full-time staff members at these churches who've never met the senior pastor. Even in small churches, pastors are consumed with being the sole preacher, counselor, administrator, and part-time janitor.

Then there is the turnover of pastors and attendees. Experiencing the same pastor-parishioner relationship for more than three years is rare. The advice you're apt to receive in church regarding how to grow spiritually is: "Attend worship services regularly"; "Get involved in a ministry to serve others"; and "Join a small group." Sermons tend to be "one size fits many," determined by the leader or lectionary schedule. Programs and events are marketed for all to attend.

Having attended church my entire life and led in it for thirty years, I'm aware of the coming and going of people in a typical congregation. Most of a pastor's life is consumed with urgent care, counseling matters, weekend message preparation, ministry management, and staff supervision. Rarely can a part- or full-time minister invest extended energy in assisting an individual in developing his or her spiritual growth plan. It is not that we're disinterested, it's just that we're consumed with providing resources and services for an entire group. We have to think about the whole more than the parts.

For years I've seen people come and go through the revolving church door. They find a faith community, are attracted to something, and come back a few times. A certain percent

get involved in a small group, socials, Bible studies, and seminars. They grow some, but most of it is helter-skelter, hit-
and-miss, random improvement. Rarely do people sit with a
pastor or spiritual mentor and think through what it is they
should be focusing on, what their next steps ought to be,
or even how a person deepens spiritually. No athlete would
ever make the Olympics with such a haphazard, willy-nilly
training strategy. Commitment alone is insufficient. Good-
heartedness does not result in a smart heart. You reap what
you sow.

You may not be an active churchgoer. A majority in the
U.S. are not, far fewer in Europe. Perhaps you don't identify
yourself as a Christian because you don't buy into a specific
set of beliefs or views. You appreciate Oprah, Deepak Chopra,
Anthony Robbins, the Dalai Lama, or any number of other
contemporary teachers. Yet you're open to learning about
Jesus out of respect for his life and teachings.

We all vary in our experiences, knowledge, strengths, challenges, and weaknesses. One size won't fit all when it comes
to spiritual next steps. As important as a community is to
spiritual growth, groups do not develop a relationship with
God. Individuals do.

Your Creator has given you the responsibility of piloting
your spiritual flight. The myth is that it's a pastor's or church's
job, but it's not. Their role is to provide growth opportunities. They create and distribute resources and services so that
you can pick and choose items for your development, but few
are specifically designed to take you where you need to go.
You're responsible for your soul, and if you're a parent with
a child at home, you're also in charge of helping your son or
daughter grow spiritually.

While such a responsibility sounds burdensome, it can
also liberate and empower. The good news is you don't have
to figure it out alone. By following the methods Jesus used
in helping those around him, you too can develop spiritual
intelligence.

Now What?

Running an effective business requires a plan. Starting a long journey without a map or sense of direction is unwise. Health experts tell us that if we want to begin an exercise program, we must develop an idea of where we're headed and what it's going to take to accomplish our goal. So why would we pursue a spiritual journey with comparatively little planning? How do we know if we're making progress? What confirmation do we have that we're working on what we need for our next step? Most people I encounter meander through life with little conscious effort in how to mature. They rely on messages crafted for entire congregations or masses of TV viewers. Then, after so many years of this, they wonder why they're not further along.

Spiritual intelligence begins by taking responsibility for your own soul growth. In this book you will learn what is involved in an intentional development plan that is personal, grounded, and effective. In over fifty years in the church, I'm aghast that no one ever sat with me and said, "Alan, here's what you need to do to develop a lifelong process of soul growth." My hit-and-miss journey has led to numerous cul-de-sacs. I've felt like a mouse in a maze. I've been frustrated, disappointed, and sometimes even shocked with my wandering.

What you won't find here is a Bible study, a list of irrefutable laws, a church's program for discipleship, or a self-help mantra to chant. What you will discover is a methodology, a grounded set of principles that will help you grow your soul. You'll be given a set of tools to assess your spiritual development and help you take the next step on your journey of spiritual growth.

If you're a pastor, teacher, lay leader, or discipler of others, you'll gain insights into how Jesus developed his followers and how you can empower those you influence to take charge of their own growth. In fact, you'll see how *your* continued growth is crucial to helping others develop.

The Learner

Jesus chose one primary term when referring to his followers. Those who chronicled his life tell us that his first twelve students were called *disciples*. This moniker referred to anyone who followed him. "Anyone who does not carry his cross and follow me cannot be my disciple" (Luke 14:27). The words *disciple* and *disciples* occur over three hundred times in the New Testament.

In the ancient method of learning, students intentionally followed their mentors and teachers, gleaning from them in a variety of settings, covering a number of issues. Today, this approach seems unrealistic for most of us. People usually refer to Jesus's followers as "Christians," a term only used three times in the New Testament (Acts 11:26; 26:28; 1 Pet. 4:16), and "born again," also found merely three times (John 3:3, 7; 1 Pet. 1:23). These words refer to a state of being and position, but do not emphasize the dynamic process of learning or growth to the same extent as "disciple." Jesus seemed to feel very comfortable with the word *disciple*, as shown by his repetitive use of it. That means for us to grow our soul Jesus's way, we must be intentional learners. Active learning is the key, not passive education or mere belief. Free will is one of your God-given qualities, but it means that only you can choose to pursue your soul growth.

A good synonym for "disciple" is "learner," which I think comes across with a bit more meaning to our twenty-first-century ears. So we're going to use the term *learner* as the name for those who are actively interested in pursuing the methods that Jesus used to grow souls. To be a learner implies humility. You never get it fully figured out. You continually, intentionally explore new ideas and grapple with them. In the Old Testament, God changed the name of Jacob to Israel, which literally means "God-wrestler." The word stuck and became the name of God's people throughout history. Apparently, God likes to wrestle. Passive intellectuals pursuing philosophical mysteries need not apply. We're interested in transformation, maturity.

Travel Plans

We have become the most travel-intensive civilization in history. Planes, trains, buses, and automobiles take us to work, vacations, shopping centers, school, parks, entertainment, and out to eat. When we haven't had enough road time, we hop in the car for a couple hours' getaway to the mountains, ocean, or countryside. Travel has become a part of who we are. So it was with Jesus. He said, "Follow me" (Matt. 4:19; 8:22; 9:9), implying he was going somewhere. He also said, "I am the Way" (John 14:6), equating his life to a path or journey.

It is hard to deny that Jesus was the most influential person in history. We know very little about him before the age of thirty. His life from that point only lasted about three years, but in that time he was constantly on the move. Jesus did not set up shop, establish a church, or hang out the shingle for those seeking his wisdom, healing, and mentoring. Jesus took his learners on a road trip. In those months of movement, they were impacted so significantly that this tiny group of learners changed the world forever.

The concept of a journey should be an easy metaphor for us to relate to. We're on a trip, traveling through life, discovering why we're here, what we're to be doing, who we're to be doing it with, and how we can leave a legacy and prepare for eternity.

Your journey is individual. No one before or after you is like you. No matter how similar or dissimilar your days look, you and your circumstances are changing. Neighbors move in and out. Jobs come and go. Technology upgrades. People enter and exit your life as strangers, familiar faces, best friends, and loved ones. Life Avenue is a busy boulevard of laughing, crying, worrying, hoping, paying bills, and pursuing goals.

You're not on your journey alone. Throughout history, most humans have recognized a Higher Power, Creator, Divine Intelligence. Those who deny such a deity tend to be those who've not yet found one in whom they can believe. God is on the road with you and has devised a process by which you can get to know your Creator, resulting in maturity and fulfillment. Jesus demonstrated this in the short time he worked with his small band of followers. By studying how Jesus did what he did, so often overlooked by traditional Christian teachers, you can tap into the powerful results of his methods.

Interaction Ideas:

1. What is a favorite trip you remember taking? What made it memorable?

2. What's the difference between being "responsible" for our soul growth and being able to grow our souls without the help of others?

3. Why do you think Jesus spent most of three years "on the road" instead of settling in one place?

4. What concerns you about the idea that you hold the steering wheel of your soul development, instead of delegating that responsibility to others?

5. When we say it's your responsibility to grow your soul, we don't mean you do it alone. Discuss your level of readiness to develop a soul growth plan for yourself that may involve other people.

Activity: Take a two- or three-inch ball of clay and shape it into a form that represents your spiritual condition or your readiness to grow spiritually. Share the meaning and significance of the shape. The Bible uses the story of a potter and clay to depict a person's relationship with God. Who do you think the potter is, and who/what does the clay represent? (It's more of a metaphor than an exact comparison, as clay is a non-living element.) How does the clay differ from humans, and where does personal responsibility come into the picture?

TWO

Soul Cartography

Assessing Your Journey
toward Spiritual Intelligence

Our family has a good friend named Pam. She helps us navigate the local, winding streets of Monterey, Carmel-by-the-Sea, and Pacific Grove, plus nonlocal cities we visit. "Pam" is the name we've given to our GPS device because of its feminine voice and because Pam is "map" in reverse. Pam tells us how to get to the destination we key in, because at any given time, thanks to satellites, she knows our present location.

Every successful trip requires two things: knowing where you are and knowing where you want to go. Assessing your current position is important. The Journey is a short tool providing a snapshot of your spiritual life. Unlike some assessments that are complicated looks at gifts, leadership, personality style, or doctrinal knowledge, The Journey combines stories, outcomes, and qualities others observe that indicate maturity. You can look at the components of The Journey in Appendix A in the back of this book, or you can download a free, full-sized copy at www.spiritualintelligence.org (not to be confused with the website ending in ".com"), along with other resources related to this book. We'll take an in-depth look in this chapter at each of the components of The Journey.

Most people never assess their spiritual growth, or they use unreliable standards (such as Sunday school pins, seminar certificates, election to a church office) that don't really reflect what they're after. A scale does not measure good health, even though weight is an important factor in health. Many assume it's not possible to establish observable benchmarks for soul growth. But if you travel on the inside, it will be evident on the outside. On the other hand, some try to measure spirituality exclusively using a list of externals, assuming that by achieving these, we prove we're growing. The problem is that you can accomplish externals without traveling internally.

A soul assessment reveals potential targets for initial growth emphasis. It also helps you establish a benchmark so that you can see where you've progressed. Like pencilmarks on a doorjamb that a parent uses to record a child's height, you can compare old feedback with new, every six to eighteen months. In order to improve the accuracy of your assessment, you'll want to solicit input from people who know you in a variety of settings (family, work, church, neighbors, community).

The differences in spiritual assessments come down to measurement preferences among the designers. Some are more knowledge-oriented, looking at what you know. Others only look at self-perceptions. And others involve personality and strength indicators. The Journey, an assessment I developed and have used over the years, is a short, four-page, user-friendly, yet relatively comprehensive response tool that you can complete to establish a benchmark. There is also a one-page survey for others to fill out about you.

Soul cartography helps us determine where we are now, where we want to go, and how we can get there. Following is a description of and instructions for The Journey, which serves as a tool for designing a soul growth plan by providing a pithy, compact view of desirable outcomes. It is based on the methods described in Section I of this book and works best in the context of a Travel Team and Path Finder (terms we will define and unpack in later chapters).

The Journey includes a section for you to tell your story and thus highlight the events that have marked your life. There is a succinct assessment of twenty SI indicators that can be provided to those who know you, so you can glean from their perspectives in addition to your own. Finally, you'll find simple directions that help you summarize your development and next steps for growth. The result is that with this information, you can develop your own soul growth plan, providing structure based on individualized goals, not just generic concepts. The Journey will not recommend specific resources or activities, but will give you insights into how you're progressing and where to invest more attention for continued growth. You may want to revise The Journey every six to eighteen months, but a nice rhythm is an annual update.

When several people within a single faith community take The Journey, the cumulative feedback allows for new programs, ministries, curriculum, and message topics to emerge. Instead of hit-or-miss planning and promoting of a new event based on staff ideas, pastors and ministry leaders can have specific people in mind, based on a cluster of The Journey reports. By using spiritual growth assessments, congregational leaders and soul developers will be better informed about the needs of the people in their care, empowering them to be more responsive. As a result, people will be less likely to plateau or feel the desire to find another church, which is often the perception when a next step is needed.

Familiarize yourself with The Journey assessment and then use the following instructions for responding to the instrument. (The downloadable version of The Journey has four full-sized pages, denoted in the following parentheses.) There are five parts of this tool:

1. Narrative Snapshot (page 1)
2. LifeLine (page 2)

3. Growth Indicator (page 3)
4. Progress Plotter (page 4A)
5. Next Steps (page 4B)

Narrative Snapshot (page 1)

This section prompts you to assess spiritual growth activities in a brief, narrative format. Four strategic questions or statements of common soul growth efforts help you create an overview of your experiences. The limited response space forces you to prioritize your answers. Writing exacts your thinking, aiding you in clarifying your ideas and experiences. While you may not think this exercise would be beneficial to do annually, especially if the past year did not seem to involve significant changes, the big picture awareness that comes from this exercise can be insightful. As we grow, our perspectives change in how we perceive marking events and prioritize defining moments in our lives.

Write a brief spiritual (church/religious) history of your life:
This item looks for more traditional means of developing your soul through organized approaches, most commonly church involvement. Some people have no formalized spiritual experience.

List your perceived strengths/gifts and serving experiences:
This instruction focuses more on involvement than mere attendance. Where have you taught, worked behind the scenes, or served people in need? How have you been involved in using your abilities to benefit others?

Spiritual/religious education/learning (who, what, when, where, how):

What kind and to what extent is your spiritual and/or religious education? These might include catechism, Sunday school, vacation Bible school, religious classes in college, small group Bible studies, or online classes or resources that go beyond inspiration.

THE JOURNEY:
A SPIRITUAL HEALTH ASSESSMENT AND DEVELOPMENT PLAN

Name _Alan E. Nelson_ Date _8.09_ Age/Gender _50 / m_
Street Address/City/State/Zip/Contact Info: _Monterey, CA_

NARRATIVE SNAPSHOT: (*Respond to the following issues as succinctly as possible.*)

Write a brief spiritual (church/religious) history of your life:

I became a Jesus follower as a young child (5), grew up in the church, & then rebelled from a call to ministry, late high school. I've maintained faith, except for a time of brokenness in my late 20s and a mid-life storm. I would say my 2nd half is unfolding well.

List your perceived strengths/gifts and serving experiences:

My strengths include training, entrepreneurial leading, writing and creativity. I have experience as a church planter.

Spiritual/religious education/learning (who, what, when, where, how):

I have an undergrad degree in biblical literature. I have attended numerous conferences and done some writing in the area of spiritual growth.

How would you describe your spiritual health the last six months?

I am experiencing a new chapter in my life after a time of feeling distant from God and questioning my upper layers of spirituality.

©2009 The Journey assessment from the book: Spiritual Intelligence by Alan E. Nelson, EdD www.spiritualintelligence.org

37

How would you describe your spiritual health the last six months?
We all have ebbs and flows in our spiritual lives. This question explores your perceived trends. Are you hot, cold, or lukewarm? What has happened in the last few months that best explains your current condition? Is the tide coming in or going out, and why do you think that?

LifeLine (page 2)

A LifeLine is an effective tool for seeing the events that have marked your life and for sharing your story and spiritual topography with someone. It is a visual depiction of where you've been and events that have helped define you. You can do a LifeLine with a crayon on paper or a sophisticated computer rendering. Determining where you are now and where you should head are often related to where you've been and what has taken place in your life. Once you've listed ten or so defining moments, you'll plot these on a grid for a visual mapping so that you can see the significant ups and downs of your story. Some people like to practice on scratch paper, because you'll want to put some thought into this process and where you plot these on the grid.

Instructions:

1. List eight to twelve significant events in your life in chronological order, from birth through the most recent. These could be spiritual, social, physical, or emotional experiences that have marked you. You may choose to include things such as: childhood trauma, divorce, choosing to follow Jesus, significant moves/jobs/relationships, spiritual breakthroughs, marriage, births, deaths, and the like. This is your choice, but work at keeping the list between eight and twelve items.

2. Write your birth year on the left end of the bottom, horizontal line. The right end is today's year. You don't have to be exact, but use the grid lines to approximate years in your time line.

3. Place dots on the graph, representing the eight to twelve events or impacts you listed. The dot on the left side in the middle of the box represents your birth. Begin at the dot and move toward the right, to the approximate time of the first occurrence on your list. Place a dot there, either above or below the middle, horizontal line, depending on whether this was a positive impact (above) or negative impact (below). The farther up or down from the midpoint you plot the dot, the more positive or negative it was. Place the number beside the dot which corresponds to the line of the written description. Occasionally, people find it helpful to place two dots on the grid for the same event, because it was both positive and negative at the same time. For example, being diagnosed with cancer may have been devastating, but as a result, you changed your priorities in life to get close to loved ones and God, so you see one item as both very negative and very positive at the same time.

4. After you've plotted the dots, representing the eight to twelve significant events, connect them with a line, so that you can see the ups and downs of your life. If you decided to plot two dots for certain items, you'll see how the spiritual aspect of your life may look somewhat different than your life in general. When things are going poorly, it's possible to experience a spiritual high, and when all appears successful on the outside, your walk with God can be in the tank. Generally, you'll have one dot per significant event.

Following is a sample LifeLine:

1. *Born to parents with faith, lived on Iowa farm, positive childhood.*
2. *Decision to follow Jesus when five and a half years old.*
3. *Moved to small town in junior high, began to withdraw from God.*
4. *Rededicated my life spring semester.*
5. *Met wife-to-be while serving in Caribbean; dreams can come true.*
6. *Wilderness period after grad school; God changing career plans.*
7. *Began church in SoCal; went through a time of brokenness.*
8. *High times: three boys born, finished a doctorate, first book published.*
9. *Career disappointment in a move to the Midwest.*
10. *Moved to Arizona to enjoy the start of a new church.*
11. *Midlife issues hit, creating family tension and inner turmoil, mom died.*
12. *Post-midlife transition resulting in growing fulfillment and productivity.*

Growth Indicator (page 3)

Credible, spiritual growth measurements are important. Without them, you wind up doing target practice like Charlie Brown, the Peanuts cartoon character. Charlie shoots arrows into his backyard fence, then walks over to them and draws a circle around each arrow. Lucy says, "Charlie, that's not how to do target practice." Charlie responds, "I know, but this way, I never miss."

"The Dow" is a stock market index that provides a sample of how certain stocks in an industry are doing. Spiritual intelligence is complex and diverse, but the Growth Indicator is similar to the Dow, looking at a sampling of characteristics

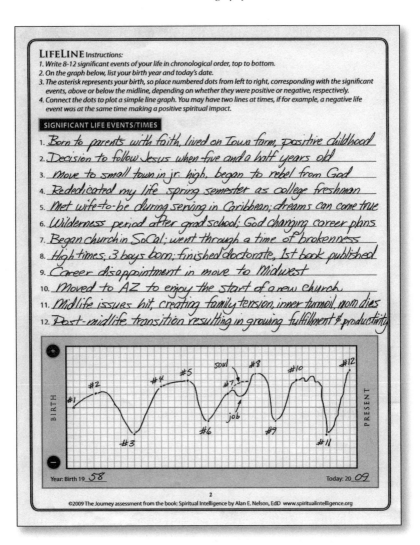

LIFELINE Instructions:
1. Write 8-12 significant events of your life in chronological order, top to bottom.
2. On the graph below, list your birth year and today's date.
3. The asterisk represents your birth, so place numbered dots from left to right, corresponding with the significant events, above or below the midline, depending on whether they were positive or negative, respectively.
4. Connect the dots to plot a simple line graph. You may have two lines at times, if for example, a negative life event was at the same time making a positive spiritual impact.

SIGNIFICANT LIFE EVENTS/TIMES

1. Born to parents with faith, lived on Town farm, positive childhood
2. Decision to follow Jesus when five and a half years old
3. Move to small town in jr. high, began to rebel from God
4. Rededicated my life spring semester as college freshman
5. Met wife-to-be during serving in Caribbean; dreams can come true
6. Wilderness period after grad school; God changing career plans
7. Began church in SoCal; went through a time of brokenness
8. High times; 3 boys born; finished doctorate, 1st book published
9. Career disappointment in move to Midwest
10. Moved to AZ to enjoy the start of a new church.
11. Midlife issues hit, creating family tension, inner turmoil, mom dies
12. Post-midlife transition resulting in growing fulfillment & productivity

Year: Birth 19 _58_   Today: 20 _09_

2

©2009 The Journey assessment from the book: Spiritual Intelligence by Alan E. Nelson, EdD www.spiritualintelligence.org

that reflect observable, measurable outcomes. Throughout time, certain character qualities, reflected in actions and attitudes, have consistently emerged as indicators of spiritual development in the lives of learners. These reflect things that Jesus taught and modeled. The Journey includes these in the Growth Indicator, assessing twenty enduring qualities for the purpose of providing a tool for benchmarking and feedback.

This instrument becomes far more effective if filled out by those who know you, since self-perceptions can be deceiving. Because spiritual fruit is revealed primarily in our relationships, those who interact with us see things that we may not. The feedback forms are modified to feel less religious or overtly spiritual, so that you can be more comfortable asking non-Christian friends to respond. Try to get responders in a variety of settings, such as church, work, family, the community, and social circles. Let responders know that their answers will remain anonymous. This is very important. If people think you'll read their responses, they will modify them, which won't benefit you. Strive to get five to ten responders, more if you're not sure how many will follow through on the survey. An alternative is to provide a longer list of potential responders and let a third-party receiver randomly select people to respond, thus reducing the chance that you'll know who provided feedback.

Instructions:

1. Read the description and if you want to, the biblical references for the qualities.
2. Consider how you emulate these traits (actions/attitudes) on a consistent basis. Rate each on a scale of 1–5 (1 rarely to nonexistent, 2 little, 3 off and on, 4 quite a bit, 5 consistently and with excellence).
3. Ask five to ten people who know you to complete this questionnaire about you. These people are referred to as responders. Try to find responders who see you in varying roles, not just a single group such as church friends. Consider those who will give you open and honest answers, not based on revenge or motivated to share only the positive. Again, this questionnaire is modified slightly from the one you take for yourself, to

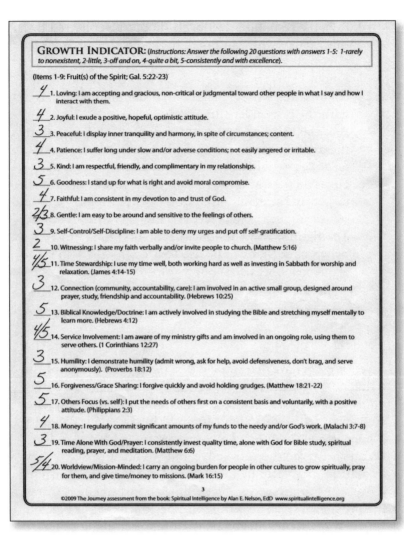

GROWTH INDICATOR: *(Instructions: Answer the following 20 questions with answers 1-5: 1-rarely to nonexistent, 2-little, 3-off and on, 4-quite a bit, 5-consistently and with excellence).*

(Items 1-9: Fruit(s) of the Spirit; Gal. 5:22-23)

_4_ 1. Loving: I am accepting and gracious, non-critical or judgmental toward other people in what I say and how I interact with them.

_4_ 2. Joyful: I exude a positive, hopeful, optimistic attitude.

_3_ 3. Peaceful: I display inner tranquility and harmony, in spite of circumstances; content.

_4_ 4. Patience: I suffer long under slow and/or adverse conditions; not easily angered or irritable.

_3_ 5. Kind: I am respectful, friendly, and complimentary in my relationships.

_5_ 6. Goodness: I stand up for what is right and avoid moral compromise.

_4_ 7. Faithful: I am consistent in my devotion to and trust of God.

_2/3_ 8. Gentle: I am easy to be around and sensitive to the feelings of others.

_3_ 9. Self-Control/Self-Discipline: I am able to deny my urges and put off self-gratification.

_2_ 10. Witnessing: I share my faith verbally and/or invite people to church. (Matthew 5:16)

_4/5_ 11. Time Stewardship: I use my time well, both working hard as well as investing in Sabbath for worship and relaxation. (James 4:14-15)

_3_ 12. Connection (community, accountability, care): I am involved in an active small group, designed around prayer, study, friendship and accountability. (Hebrews 10:25)

_5_ 13. Biblical Knowledge/Doctrine: I am actively involved in studying the Bible and stretching myself mentally to learn more. (Hebrews 4:12)

_4/5_ 14. Service Involvement: I am aware of my ministry gifts and am involved in an ongoing role, using them to serve others. (1 Corinthians 12:27)

_3_ 15. Humility: I demonstrate humility (admit wrong, ask for help, avoid defensiveness, don't brag, and serve anonymously). (Proverbs 18:12)

_5_ 16. Forgiveness/Grace Sharing: I forgive quickly and avoid holding grudges. (Matthew 18:21-22)

_5_ 17. Others Focus (vs. self): I put the needs of others first on a consistent basis and voluntarily, with a positive attitude. (Philippians 2:3)

_4_ 18. Money: I regularly commit significant amounts of my funds to the needy and/or God's work. (Malachi 3:7-8)

_3_ 19. Time Alone With God/Prayer: I consistently invest quality time, alone with God for Bible study, spiritual reading, prayer, and meditation. (Matthew 6:6)

_5/4_ 20. Worldview/Mission-Minded: I carry an ongoing burden for people in other cultures to grow spiritually, pray for them, and give time/money to missions. (Mark 16:15)

3

©2009 The Journey assessment from the book: Spiritual Intelligence by Alan E. Nelson, EdD www.spiritualintelligence.org

make it more responder-friendly. If a responder does not know the answer to a question, he or she can leave it blank, but too many blanks will invalidate the entire feedback survey on the premise that the person may not know you well enough to provide valuable input for your growth.

4. Reliable responder feedback should be collected by a third party who can tabulate the results for you confidentially. Consider a Travel Team member or Path Finder. This trusted person should receive mailed or emailed responses. Include that contact information with the responder survey.

5. Ask the third party to add the totals and determine the average rating for each characteristic. Responder feedback should not include any individual names.

6. Focus on the lower value items that can serve as growth targets in future months. Don't worry about the exact scores as much as the specific areas you want to improve. Taking the Growth Indicator the first time provides a benchmark that can be used for comparison in six to eighteen months, to see how you are growing and where you may want to focus future attention.

Progress Plotter (page 4A)

Psychologists have determined that people have multiple intelligence quotients. Typical IQ tests only measure two of approximately six recognized aptitude areas. The same is true spiritually. You cannot lump SI into a single category. We've all met people who seem extremely developed in a certain area, such as knowledge, only to be surprised by how immature they seem in another area, such as relationships. If we want to grow, we'll be willing to investigate our own inconsistencies. This section of The Journey looks at four spiritual quotient categories, each representing a potential growth area.

The Four Primary Spiritual Intelligence Categories

Knowledge has to do with proper theology, doctrinal awareness, and biblical savvy, and is often content oriented. Progress in this quotient includes having adequate resources such as

Bible studies, reading, and learning from gifted teachers. (I call these resources "Directions," which will be discussed further in chapters three and five.) Knowledge alone will not result in spiritual maturity, but it is helpful, much like knowing directions assists you in finding a location on a trip.

Attitude has to do with personal outlook, emotional intelligence, and psychological disposition. Progress in this category involves God's influence on your ability to manage your emotions, establish a healthy self-image, and develop coping skills that allow you to move forward, regardless of circumstances. Attitudes alone are not sufficient to establish maturity, but they are both means and results of soul growth.

Behaviors have to do with physical manifestations of your faith, actions, habits, and conduct, both private and public. Progress in this quotient is caused by obedience, training, feedback, self-discipline, accountability, modeling, and mentoring. Actions divorced from attitudes over time create a divided self and hinder maturity.

Relationships are the category of social interaction—how you get along with others in the various spheres of your life. Progress in this quotient is often a result of God's influence, combined with emotional maturity, self-esteem, temperament, and past experiences. While emotional and chemical issues can reduce capacity, spiritual development can maximize your capabilities.

Each of the four categories is in a certain developmental phase at any given moment. While appearing to be linear in the chart, each has fluid connections in that you can move up or down, based on personal dynamics, free-will responses to information, and growth circumstances. When we assess the phase of each of the four quotients, we begin to grasp a greater understanding of what the Bible refers to as knowing

Jesus as "Lord." The goal is to submit to Jesus's leadership in all arenas of our lives, resulting in SI.

Five Developmental Phases

1. **Recognition phase:** We become aware of our own soul and/or fundamental basics of what following Jesus is about (engaged in growth).
2. **Reorientation phase:** We begin to see the differences between life with Jesus and without, and we start to develop this relationship more actively (fragile/up and down).
3. **Reorganization phase:** We start making intentional, obvious decisions in terms of values and lifestyle that reflect biblical guidelines (stable).
4. **Recentering phase:** We have transcended the primary struggle of who is first in our lives and begin to live out Spirit-led attitudes and behaviors (strong).
5. **Reinvesting phase:** We exude the attitude of Jesus a majority of the time and display spiritual maturity, actively mentoring others directly and indirectly (deep).

Assess which phase you are in for each of the four quotients. You now have a Progress Plotter that provides a visual overview of how you see your areas of strength and weakness. If you do not care to use the five phases for plotting your growth or strengths, you can resort to a 1–5 scale, where 1 is low and 5 is high. Growth emphases can be determined by the areas where you need to see improvement. Once you have determined the categories you want to target for growth, you can combine this with the information gained from the Growth Indicator. For example, in the attitude category, you may want to focus on attitudes of humility and optimism, using knowledge tools for studying about these in Scripture and other writings and teachings. These qualities may be the focus in an accountability group (called a Travel

Team) much like an athlete builds strength by focusing his workout on a certain part of his body. The Progress Plotter is also a helpful communication tool to present your spiritual growth goals to others for feedback and to brainstorm exercise ideas.

PROGRESS PLOTTER: (We express our spiritual growth in four primary arenas. Rate yourself on a 1-5 scale in each of these areas, per the defined levels.)

	Knowledge: Awareness of Bible content, doctrine, and knowing how to study Scriptures and discern God's truth.	Attitudes: How we handle our emotions and responses to circumstances.	Behavior: The way we act in terms of moral & lifestyle issues; deeds, works.	Relationships: The quality of our social interactions; love, peace, forgiveness, giving grace, and serving others.
Level 5: Pouring yourself into others so that they mature because of your influence.	✕			
Level 4: Strong on your own; able to respond well as issues arise in this area.			✕	
Level 3: Generally stable in this area; showing growth but noted areas for improvement.		✕		✕
Level 2: Up and down; unsure where you'll be from day to day; generally unstable.				
Level 1: Struggling; some major challenges in this area that are negatively affecting your soul.				

Next Steps: (Prayerfully and possibly with the help of a Path Finder or spiritually mature assistant, write out a realistic plan for spiritual growth, which might include specific events, programs, weekly disciplines, study areas, and/or accountability relationships which will make this realistic. Review the plan regularly and re-take The Journey in 6-18 months.)
Path Finder/mentor's name: ___*Journey Group*___

What were your lower Spiritual Intelligence Plotter cell(s) and 3-5 lowest Soul Growth Indicator items that showed up in your self-evaluation or feedback from others?

Teaching: What do you need to study in the coming weeks/months to address these issues? How will you obtain adequate teaching in these areas?

Accountability: What small group or individual can you make a covenant with to hold you accountable for growth in these specific areas? How will you establish accountability?

Mentor/model: Who can you establish a mentoring relationship with who might help you grow in these specific areas? Who can you mentor in order to help them grow as well as stretching yourself?

Experience: What experiential events or commitments can you develop that will help you to grow in these areas? List times, events, deadlines, and other details:

4

©2009 The Journey assessment from the book: Spiritual Intelligence by Alan E. Nelson, EdD www.spiritualintelligence.org

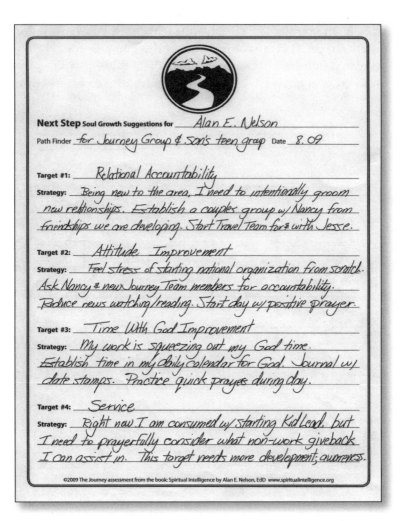

Next Step Soul Growth Suggestions for _Alan E. Nelson_

Path Finder _for Journey Group & Son's teen group_ Date _8.09_

Target #1: _Relational Accountability_

Strategy: _Being new to the area, I need to intentionally groom new relationships. Establish a couples group w/ Nancy from friendships we are developing. Start Travel Team for & with Jesse._

Target #2: _Attitude Improvement_

Strategy: _Feel stress of starting national organization from scratch. Ask Nancy & new Journey Team members for accountability. Reduce news watching/reading. Start day w/ positive prayer._

Target #3: _Time With God Improvement_

Strategy: _My work is squeezing out my God time. Establish time in my daily calendar for God. Journal w/ date stamps. Practice quick prayers during day._

Target #4: _Service_

Strategy: _Right now I am consumed w/ starting KidLead, but I need to prayerfully consider what non-work giveback I can assist in. This target needs more development; awareness._

©2009 The Journey assessment from the book: Spiritual Intelligence by Alan E. Nelson, EdD www.spiritualintelligence.org

Next Steps (page 4B)

Whether you use the assistance of spiritual mentor and peers, you are responsible for developing your own Journey plan. Aim for a simple one- to two-page response to The Journey information and be as detailed as possible. The fact that you've thought through a planning process will put you far ahead of most. As we noted earlier, research shows that the process of writing and articulating your plans heightens the likelihood that you'll implement them.

The Journey is a simple diagnostic instrument for communication, designed to help you develop a personal soul growth plan. If you find one that works better, use it, but be sure to do it in the context of the methods Jesus used, if you want to acquire SI.

Interaction Ideas:

1. Have everyone complete The Journey. Take fifteen to twenty minutes during each gathering time for one person to share his or her LifeLine. After each time, provide five minutes for group members to ask questions, share their perceptions, and affirm the individual for sharing his or her LifeLine.

2. Why do you think having an instrument like The Journey is helpful?

3. What is it about certain events that seem to mark us? What were common qualities in the points we listed on our LifeLine graphs?

4. In your experience, which of the four methods tended to be overutilized and/or underutilized (page 4B)? What were some results of this?

Activity: Take a map and select a location that most in your team would be unfamiliar with, or print a MapQuest page of a popular site. Determine two to three possible routes of how to get there from where you are presently. Then ask for stories of road trips gone awry, where you or someone in your group got lost. If you're really daring, get in your cars and go on a road trip, providing only directions or a drawing but no final location. Then talk about the importance in having milestones on trips and why tools like The Journey are helpful spiritually. What are mile markers that some use to measure their soul growth and how are these effective or not?

THREE

Jesus's Soul Growth Method

Why Most Spiritual Activities Don't Get Us
Where We Want to Go

Now that you've had an opportunity to do some soul cartography with The Journey, hopefully you'll be even more inspired to learn how it is you can navigate the next phase of your spiritual walk. At the moment, I'm writing in a beautiful chapel in Carmel-by-the-Sea called The Church of the Wayfarer. It's a small but exquisite sanctuary with stained-glass windows and the sound of wind chimes outside, just a few blocks from Carmel Beach and Pebble Beach Golf Course. If you lived in New York and wanted to get here, you could fly into Monterey airport, but then you'd need to rent a car or take a taxi the remainder of the way. An airplane will only get you so far.

Churches, both very traditional and ultracontemporary, typically provide an array of methods that help us grow spiritually. They vary in style, content, anointing, and effectiveness. But if your ultimate destination is maturity, or high SI, then chances are you'll need to incorporate a different means to arrive at your destination. It need not be in place of what got you where you are, but it will likely need to be in addition to it.

Over the years, I've met people who reminded me of Jesus. They didn't look like the drawings I've seen, but they sure seemed like him in their character. But I often wonder why *more* people don't remind me of Jesus. Some suggest it's because of the resilient power of the old nature (sin). Could it be the inadequacy of the gospel or God's Spirit to liberate us from this negative influence? Does God make a difference, and if so, how much?

What if the flaw is in the method by which we've gone about spiritual growth? What if the secret to soul development has been right under our noses all the time, but because we've replicated and merely updated what has been passed to us, we've missed it?

Life is full of traditions carried from the past, with little thought about their pertinence. For example, do you know why the two rails on a railroad track are the distance they are from each other? The source dates back to Roman chariots. The wheels created such deep ruts in the roads that all chariots began to be built with the same axle width, so as not to break them. This same width was used when building the early rail system and has continued over the years.

Religious organizations are no different. Many practices and routines exist that we assume have biblical bases, but are little more than traditions perpetuated from preceding generations. Years ago I wrote a book with Gene Appel called *How to Change Your Church (Without Killing It)*. Our research showed how difficult it is to bring about change in an established congregation. Even Jesus noted this tendency in his day to perpetuate the familiar over what is right: "You have a fine way of setting aside the commands of God in order to observe your own traditions!" (Mark 7:9). Ultimately, Jesus's disregard for some of the religious traditions of his day resulted in his crucifixion.

Jesus's Secret Sauce

During college I worked my way through school as a ventriloquist. I'd perform at public school assemblies, birthday parties, children's rallies, and church services. People paid for the dummy, and sometimes they'd let me speak as well. Ventriloquism is little more than audio magic. It relies on sleight of voice instead of sleight of hand. Like magic, ventriloquism depends on misdirection. Our ears are poor direction sensors, so when the ventriloquist talks without moving his lips and the dummy moves its lips, our eyes automatically focus on the movement, making us think the dummy is alive.

While I'm sure it was never Jesus's goal to misdirect us, that's what has happened. People focus on what he said (his teachings and conversations) and what he did (his healings, travels, and miracles) far more than *how* or *why* he did them. Most churches and Christian ministries look at the *what*. But the secret sauce of his life transformation is in the *how*. If you want to discover the way Jesus changed lives in such a short time, study his methods.

A majority believe in the divinity of Jesus. Orthodox Christianity teaches that he shared DNA with God. If this is true, he'd certainly know the best way to accomplish his goals. Assuming Jesus realized he had limited time, he'd naturally choose methods that would prove the most effective in the shortest time possible.

Misdirection is a result of inordinate emphasis on Christian teaching and programs that lack the ability to transform. We assume the power is in the *what*, but *what* without *how* is little more than religious traditions that provide a semblance of spiritual activity and development, yielding limited results. We need the secret sauce.

Spiritual intelligence is a natural result when you implement the methods Jesus used. By *natural*, I don't mean a guarantee. Farmers know there are no certainties in their work. Too much relies on weather, germination, seed hybrid, soil type, and a dozen other variables. Even Jesus didn't bat a thousand when it came to developing mature learners. Judas never got it. Free will means every individual holds the steering wheel of his or her soul. Life experiences can become inhibitors to our emotional and spiritual development. But if we want to uncover the ingredients in Jesus's secret sauce, we must join him on his journey of how he grew the souls of those around him.

Jesus did not establish a central platform from which to operate. He never built a building, formed a board, or established a budget. You can't say he created any programs, wrote any books, or did much of what we think of today as ways to grow our souls. For three years, Jesus was pretty much on a road trip.

Jesus used a combination of four primary methods. We'll introduce them briefly, and then more fully in the following four chapters. They are not necessarily in a sequential order; rather, they work together.

Travel Team

The first thing Jesus did was gather a Travel Team. He personally invited twelve individuals to go with him on a three-year journey. The genius of this method is that twelve is about the largest group you can form where there can be intimacy, accountability, and participation. More than a dozen and it becomes unwieldy. Group dynamics change significantly. Among the Twelve, three were a sort of inner circle with whom Jesus invested more time—this included John, Peter, and James. Jesus's approach to soul growth requires that we participate in a Travel Team of four to twelve, with the implicit purpose of doing life together, which includes spiritual interaction and soul growth.

This is not a shopping clique, softball team, fishing group, or happy-hour club. You may do all or none of those things, but when it comes to spiritual growth, the idea is to journey together with a few people willing to invest in a sacred adventure. At the same time, it's not a Bible study or typical small group, which is why most of these fail to result in significant impact. There must be elements of experiencing life and mission together. We will take a closer look at the Travel Team in the next chapter.

Directions

When you are driving through a new city, having good directions is important, whether it is a map or GPS device. None of us have visited life before, so we need information that transcends our limited guidance system. Directions involve input from God that is reliable for making spiritually healthy decisions, as well as inspiration and revealing the nature of God.

Jesus continually sought Directions in his life. He frequently arose early or stayed up late to talk with God. Jesus also relied on holy writings. History points out that as early as age twelve, he discussed Scriptures in the temple with the rabbis. Throughout his ministry, he quoted various passages from what we refer to today as the Old Testament. We don't see Jesus making it up as he went or merely quoting popular sages.

At the same time, the disciples continually received Directions from Jesus. Many of Jesus's words became content in the New Testament. These ideas influenced others (e.g., Peter, James, and Paul) who provided further Directions that have been deemed holy and reliable.

Just as there are physical laws of nature, there are spiritual ones. Someone said, "You can't break the laws of nature, but you can break yourself against the laws of nature." The same is true spiritually.

The purpose of reliable Directions, such as Bible study, sound teaching, and complementary info and inspiration, is to avoid winging it or relying solely on your own instincts. Sharing ideas or getting opinions from someone else isn't sufficient. Jesus's method of getting and giving Directions was an important part of how he helped grow the souls of his followers. We'll discuss this further in chapter five, which will include practical ideas on assessing the sources of your Directions.

Experiencing the Trip

Jesus's three-year journey with his Travel Team was experiential, providing on-the-job training. Unlike traditional church programs in which we seclude ourselves in a classroom for a passive, intellectual contemplation about God and scriptural teachings, Jesus used active learning methodology. He knew that people learn best by doing. He continually created opportunities for the learners to experience what he was striving to teach. They were on a mission, not on the couch talking about mission.

Jesus's interactions with large crowds can be seen as opportunities for the learners to see how he served and lived. They provided experience for them in the same area. Passive learning methods provide little traction for Directions to take hold in our lives. People rarely change until they perceive a reason for learning a concept or action. Experience is to learning what water is to a seed, allowing it to sprout, take root, and grow. We'll further discuss this idea of Experiencing the Trip in chapter six.

Path Finder

Sometimes we overlook the obvious. We acknowledge that Jesus was more than merely a dispenser of information and knowledge. He was a teacher in the Eastern sense, which meant that he provided wisdom for how the Directions work in life and how one might avoid falling into a ditch on the trip. This aspect of the method is what we call a Path Finder, which we will explore further in chapter seven. The title fits

the metaphor of this book, but also helps us avoid more traditional ideas of coach, mentor, spiritual director, or consultant.
A Path Finder is all of these and yet different.

Path Finding is what Jesus did intuitively. John wrote, "the
Word became flesh" (John 1:14). The idea of incarnation,
a truth or concept becoming tangible, is at the root of Path
Finding. When you're visiting a new city and ask a local for
directions to a certain park or neighborhood, the response you
often get is a description of topography and landmarks. The
Path Finder helps the person move toward a destination, but
the driver is still on his own to figure it out experientially.

Jesus was a Path Finder for his Travel Team. Then eleven
of the Twelve became Path Finders for others. Your journey
of spiritual intelligence should include a Path Finder. At the
start you have one. In the middle you have one and are one.
Toward the end you are one.

Synergy

Synergy results when everything working together is greater
than the sum of the individual parts. Synergy is what happens
in a good recipe. If you're making chocolate chip cookies, it's
good to work from a recipe. Leave out a main ingredient such
as flour, sugar, chocolate chips, or butter, and it changes the
outcome of a great cookie. Put too much salt in the mixing
bowl and you'll hear, "Yuck, these cookies are salty." Eaten
individually, the recipe ingredients don't taste like a cookie.
But combine them in the right amounts and bake them in
the oven, and you have a delicious treat.

While soul growth isn't a recipe, there is a synergistic effect
that shouldn't be overlooked. Although we've identified four
methods that Jesus used for growing souls, the title of this
chapter is singular: "Jesus's Soul Growth Method." That's
because he seamlessly interwove all four into a single strand,
resulting in his unique and powerful method. We break these

apart in order to understand the dynamics of each, but unless they are implemented together, they will not have their full effect. Here are examples of what tends to happen when one or more of the four are out of balance.

Too heavy or too light on Directions

Many people focus on getting Directions, becoming extremely intelligent map readers. Seminaries, Bible colleges, and church pews teem with people who know the Bible inside and out. They can parse the Greek, quote verses, and explain doctrinal distinctions between Reformed Calvinists, Wesleyan-Armenians, and Charismatics. But apart from a Travel Team, Experience, and Path Finding, these people become mere biblical brainiacs. Scriptural sages delude themselves into thinking that quantity of information is the equivalent of maturity. Passionless parishioners abound, possessing little drive for God and lacking behaviors reflecting faith. Judgmentalism, religious arguing, self-righteous attitudes, and heartless ritualism are common symptoms of those who accentuate Directions over the other methods.

Yet learners who lack good Direction are susceptible to getting lost, taking paths that seem right but do not lead to spiritual maturity. Numerous religions and counter-Jesus belief systems find their best followers among people lacking good Directions. These people are vulnerable, wandering through life without a compass.

Too heavy or too light on Travel Team

People who invest too heavily in the Travel Team tend to have a lot of fun, but often find little purpose. They are also prone to exclude others. As long as they have their small mix of friends, that's all that matters. Ingrown individuals lack the benefit of insights that those outside their sphere of interest can bring. Socializing without intentional, mutual spiritual emphasis does not significantly increase SI.

The problem with not developing a Travel Team is that you rarely apply what you learn. A lack of accountability from those who know and love us results in wasted Directions. Left to our own devices, humans are incredibly undisciplined in the arena of soul growth. Self-centeredness takes over, resulting in a sense of loneliness, so that we fail to enjoy the process. A busy social schedule is not the same as a Travel Team. Sociologists talk about "crowded loneliness"—being surrounded by people, but intimate with none. Flitting around faith-oriented social engagements without a Travel Team in place will yield little long-term soul growth.

Too heavy or too light on Experiencing the Trip

The person who overemphasizes Experiencing the Trip runs the risk of emotionalism or pharisaism. Our emotions are important, but unreliable as the primary source of our guidance. Spiritual vertigo sets in, so that we think we're flying in the right direction, only to find ourselves upside down. Emotionalism can lead to an attitude of spiritual superiority. "I worship better than you. I'm closer to God than you. I speak in tongues and you don't. Tsk. Tsk. Tsk." The noncharismatic version of this is good-deed spirituality. The result is a pharisaical attitude that looks down on anyone who is not as holy, pious, or involved.

A lack of Experiencing the Trip results in faith that is little more than intellectual ascent. Experiencing the Trip produces emotional glue that causes the Directions to stick to us. We retain far less without this glue. Faith merely becomes an intellectual pursuit, lacking personal inspiration as well as the ability to excite others on their journey.

Too heavy or too light on Path Finding

When a person relies too heavily on a Path Finder, he or she is at risk of being manipulated by that person. It is possible to set people up as veritable idols. In 1 Corinthians 1:12–13, people argued about whether their Path Finder was Apollos, Paul, or Cephas. Placing too much allegiance on another person renders your faith vulnerable, should that person fall or become overly controlling.

Conversely, when you become another's Path Finder and the person relies too heavily on you, you become vulnerable to pride and seeking too much control of the other person.

On the other hand, the person avoiding a Path Finder will grow more slowly and is at risk of enduring unnecessary pain that can sabotage his or her spiritual journey. A Path Finder helps a person avoid certain potholes and dangerous curves in the road.

A person who never becomes a Path Finder will nearly always plateau spiritually. There comes a critical point in our journey where we begin learning more by teaching and developing others. When we fail to invest in others, our growth subsides, regardless of how many more Directions we procure. We also hold back those who could benefit from what we have to offer.

	Directions	Travel Team	Experiences	Path Finding
Too Heavy	• Judgmental • Confuses knowledge with application / academic • Self-righteous	• Lack of purpose • Exclusive / closed to "outsiders" • Confuses Christian fellowship with maturity	• Emotionalism / entertainment driven • Spiritual pride • Pharisaic / judgmental / good deeds driven	• Vulnerable to manipulation • Hero worship • Path Finder control and pride
Too Light	• Vulnerable to heresy • Wandering • Up and down spiritually due to lack of grounding	• Low application due to nil accountability • Self-centered • Lonely	• Intellectualism • Low retention • Little passion	• Slow growth • Unnecessary pain • Hit-and-miss searching • Consumerism (by not becoming a Path Finder)

Summing it up . . .

Whether you're traveling from New York to Carmel-by-the-Sea, or going to the moon, you're going to need appropriate modes of transportation. Typical means of spiritual growth can take us only so far. The way we get to SI is by applying Jesus's methods with diligence and intentionality.

Interaction Ideas:

1. What are two or three examples of synergy, situations where various parts need to come together in order for the outcome to be more significant than the individual parts?

2. Why do you think traditional church programming does not seem to reflect the same methods that Jesus used with the Twelve?

3. Which of the four methods seems most intriguing to you and why?

4. As you look at the graph depicting risks of too little or too much of the methods, what situations do you think are most common among the people you know? Why do you think this?

Activity: Make a batch of cookies but bake four slightly different variations. For example, leave the sugar out of one small batch, add a lot of salt to another, mix too much or too little flour into a third, and sprinkle a fourth group with garlic or onion seasoning. Keep each of the groups separate and then provide a taste test. Discuss why it's important to get the right proportion of ingredients in a recipe for it to turn out well. You can do a variation of this by over- or undercooking cupcakes.

FOUR

The Travel Team

Tapping the Power of a Spiritual Journey Group and Enjoying It

Spiritual intelligence, Jesus-style, requires a Travel Team consisting of a personally selected group of people committed to journeying together for the primary purpose of spiritual growth.

One of the first things we notice in the Gospels about Jesus's ministry is how informal it was. No buildings, budgets, or bulletins. While lacking formality, it was very intentional and strategic. He quickly assembled a group of handpicked individuals who gave up their agendas in order to learn the ways of the spiritual realm amidst the physical one.

Jesus did not travel alone. Even though others would seemingly slow him down, limit his mass impact, and entangle his plans, Jesus picked a handful of men to journey with him for the rest of his earthly life. Notice that Jesus did not issue a general "y'all come" invitation; he handpicked a dozen road trip buddies. He also did not wait for a group of people to come to him; he went after them. Note too that he did not shop in the logical places, such as the local temple or rabbinical schools. Instead, Jesus went to the workplace, seashore, and other nonreligious venues. He continued in this vein, showing his disciples that spiritual activity is not confined to certain designated times and locations. Soul growth is far more encompassing than an hour or two in the synagogue on the Sabbath.

Jesus risked being accused of favoritism! He prioritized long-term impact by choosing to go deep with a few. *More with less is still more.* Think laser instead of floodlight. Typical spiritual pursuits involve dabbling in a variety of things, with little thought about residual impact. The bottom line is blurry at best. We nibble our way through a smorgasbord of offerings, culminating in a number of tastings and a few preferences. We become soul shopaholics, consuming more but growing only a bit.

For three years Jesus and the Twelve became part of the Palestinian landscape, camping out and foraging from village to village. Word of mouth spread, attracting crowds who listened to Jesus's teaching and hoped to see a miracle (Matt. 5:1–2). But apart from a few grandstand events, most of Jesus's time was invested with this intimate group of confidants. We periodically see him trying to thin out the followers (John 6:25–66; Luke 18:18–29), avoid crowds (Mark 1:35–38), and dismiss the many (Matt. 8:18–22; 14:23). I can't imagine a pastor in America who wouldn't dream of such a problem—being bombarded with people wanting to touch his garment and listen to his teachings. But Jesus seems to have seen large groups in ways that transcend the obvious. At times they were distractions from his main business of maturing the souls of his Travel Team. At other times they provided a laboratory in which to train his learners.

Even though people wanted to promote Jesus (Matt. 21:1–11), he often avoided the limelight, suggesting at times that they not tell anyone what they'd witnessed (Matt. 8:4; 16:20; Luke 9:21). Instead, Jesus kept coming back to the Twelve, going deep with a few instead of remaining shallow with the many. Developing a Travel Team to participate in will be equally important for your own spiritual development.

In Exodus 18, when God was organizing his chosen people, Moses divided the entire nation into groups of ten. In Acts 2, people met in homes, and the average Palestinian house would likely hold less than thirty people at capacity. During early persecution, followers of Jesus met in the Roman catacombs, burial grounds where the Romans feared going. Anyone who has toured these knows their size prevented large gatherings. Throughout history, Jesus's followers have gathered in small groups while strengthening in faith. Modern China has seen a proliferation of the underground church. Contemporary America, at a time when churches are getting larger, is also seeing a revival in the house and organic (micro) church movement.

Most churches are best known for their public worship services, probably because these are the easiest means for an outsider to visit. These larger, more formal gatherings require less commitment from regulars, providing a modicum of learning and growth opportunities, but without the chafing that periodically arises when accountability takes place. This provides a venue for the most gifted teachers and musicians to serve us with their gifts. There is nothing wrong with this, so long as it is part of and not the substitute for our primary means of soul growth.

Accountability

The primary benefit of a Travel Team is that it enables us to apply spiritually oriented truths we'll call "Directions" (chapter five) that empower us to grow in the necessary areas. This happens primarily by creating an environment of nurturing accountability. The inherent goal of accountability is to improve "ability." This comes most effectively and efficiently when it is done in a social context with an intimate group holding us intentionally but informally responsible for using what we've learned.

For several years I had a problem keeping my weight down, until my friend Tom Dobyns and I began running together at 6:00 every other morning. I can't remember a morning that I yearned to run, but I'd show up anyway because I knew Tom would be waiting for me. He admitted the same. There's something powerful about two or more people committed to helping each other accomplish a task, creating positive peer pressure as a brace, much like you wrap a bum knee. Alcoholics Anonymous has built a worldwide support system on the principle, as has every winning sports team.

Unfortunately, most sermons and Bible teaching lead to little life change because they do not result in methods that catalyze transformation. Individualism works against soul growth, and let's face it, we like our independence. We resist team thinking or accountability. But when the Bible says, "You are the body of Christ" (1 Cor. 12:27), the word *you* is plural. We typically infer *you* in the Bible as singular, because we tend to think more like lone rangers than community members, but the word is often plural. This is not some neurotic "I'm incomplete without you" program of codependence; it is the reality that we can never reach maturity on our own without engaging help from others.

Realizing this, many churches provide a variety of small group options, such as Sunday school classes, Bible studies, and home groups. In many cases these groups amount to the tail wagging the dog. Jesus periodically provided large gathering venues, but he began with, ended with, and consistently maintained his Travel Team. As we'll see in a moment, the typical small group does not provide sufficient focus and accountability for us to gain what we need for maturity, which is why most participants never reach escape velocity, even though they're headed in the right direction.

Unless someone is looking for growth and application in the context of trusted community, it's probably not going to happen. The adage applies here, "don't expect what you don't inspect." We do not triumph because we don't "try *umph*."

On our own, we lack ability. We cannot muster the power it takes to become mature and certainly not to maintain a semblance of maturity over time. Although we're ultimately responsible for our own soul growth, we can't do it by ourselves. Even if you're praying, reading your Bible, listening to sermons, serving, going to church, and attending a typical class or small group, you'll only grow to a certain extent, and then you'll plateau. I've seen it hundreds if not thousands of times. We need a close circle of friends—a Travel Team—with a spiritual intent to get us where we need to go. That's one of the most difficult things to admit as a type A male who is also an only child. Self-sufficiency is high on my list, but God never created us to mature that way.

Jesus rarely operated alone. He traveled with a consistent Team. Although the primary reason for you to have a Travel Team is accountability, it's not just any type of accountability. The effective kind is what I call "Mutually Earned Accountability." Let's take a closer look at different possible levels of accountability.

Levels of Accountability

Level 1: Casual (informal, friendly, congenial, low expectations)

This level is common among a simple group of friends and nominal acquaintances. When you return from a trip, someone might say, "Hey, we missed you. How have you been?" Membership in these social circles is informal and haphazard. They consist of the regulars in a bar, work associates, members in a spinning class at the athletic club, or those who sit around you in church worship services. People may know your face and your name, but expectations are low and often superficial. That's okay. We need and enjoy these interactions, but this level of accountability will not result in significant life change.

Level 2: Convictional (informal, intentional, low to medium expectations)

As relationships grow, they naturally develop higher accountability. This level is quite common in home Bible studies, ministry teams, and more intentional affinity groups. People know something about us and will often follow up if we're absent, sick, or need help. While we're open to social interaction, the unwritten agreement is that participants have not earned the right to interfere or hold each other accountable.

Level 3: Covenant (mutually earned, intentional, voluntary, medium to high expectations)

Accountability reaches a significant level at this point because a formal agreement has been established that supports commitment to each other in a group. This is a Travel Team quality that usually requires intentional commitment. Sometimes you need to go through Levels 1 and 2 before making that commitment; rarely will Level 3 transpire on its own. The Bible is filled with metaphors of covenantal relationships, such as marriage, sacrifices, circumcision, baptism, communion, and ceremonies. It is the fabric of the proclamation of Ruth to Naomi, "Where you go I will go, and where you stay I will stay. Your people will be my people and your God my God" (Ruth 1:16). The same is seen in Jesus's invitation to his disciples: "Follow me" (Matt. 4:19) and is missing in the responses of those who needed to first take care of business and tend to an aging relative (Matt. 8:21–22).

Level 4: Concerted (formal, usually one-way, structured, voluntary, high expectations)

The level of accountability at this point borders on professional therapy. A person focused on losing weight, kicking a bad habit, confronting an identified weakness, or creating a temporary pressure for growth may voluntarily contract with a friend, therapist, coach, or group for the purpose of being held accountable in a specific area. People seeking this level on an emotional-spiritual level may join a strict religious order.

Level 5: Controlled (formal, one-way, extremely structured, involuntary, very high expectations)

Scared Straight, halfway houses, boot camp programs, and prisons are perhaps the ultimate means of accountability. These are one-way and seek to break the will and change the behavior of the participant.

The reason for clarifying these five levels is to explain why most spiritual growth structures do not result in sufficient accountability to catalyze change. A Travel Team consists of a Covenant level that fosters an environment for Mutually Earned Accountability.

MEA

Mutually Earned Accountability (MEA) is needed to catalyze SI and significant life change. Think of it like snowman snow. As I write this, there's a spring snow falling on the front range in northern Colorado. When snow is too wet and mushy, you can't make a good snowman. And when the temperature is too low, the snow is powdery and won't stick together. Any kid in cold country knows there's a consistency that's just right for making a snowball, rolling it large, and then packing it to make the snowman solid. Similarly, there's an environment that is just right for accountability to stick, resulting in personal growth toward maturity.

Mutually Earned Accountability consists of a combination of three ingredients: Emotional investment, shared trust, and personal familiarity.

Emotional investment refers to a deep level of interaction that transcends intellectual ascent. When we've positively invested in a person, we earn emotional credits. These credits are used or withdrawn when we ask favors, require patience, or need to confront the other person. A line of credit is established when we believe that future interactions with a person will ultimately yield a positive payoff. When people overextend their credit, we terminate the relationship, or at least suspend it, until a positive balance can be reestablished.

We've all experienced people speaking into our lives who did not earn that right. They were sideline critics or acquaintances who did not invest in us adequately before giving their opinion. They are some of the most challenging people, because they appear friendly but behave unkindly. They are "well-intentioned dragons," those who mean well but have not earned the right to enter our sacred soul space.

Failure to earn emotional trust is the single biggest reason why people reject faith in Jesus. They've had too many experiences with people claiming to be Jesus-followers who telegraph an attitude of self-righteousness and condemnation. "You think and behave the wrong way. You need what I have. Change." People feel judged by those who've done little to pay the price required to share such information. Jesus's teachings were usually accompanied and often preceded by giving, whether it be a healing, miracle, or feeding.

The concept is like banking. In order to withdraw cash from your ATM, you need to either have money in your account or an arranged line of credit. Giving, serving, and conveying authentic care toward people are means of making emotional deposits and opening lines of credit. Challenging their beliefs or encouraging them to risk faith represents withdrawals. Unless we've established a positive balance, we've not earned the right to make a withdrawal.

Shared trust refers to a mutual sense of dependability, predictability, and honor. This often requires time, because we can only predict another's behavior after we've had sufficient observation over a range of situations. This includes giving and receiving potentially damaging information on each other without feeling betrayed. When I share a small secret, feel accepted, and do not hear about it later from someone else, trust is established. Then I'll be willing to share a medium secret. When we don't have sufficient shared trust in our lives, we often seek professionals, such as pastors, therapists, and lawyers, who are obliged to ethical and legal codes to hold our secrets in confidence.

But "shared" means that everyone in a given relationship shares. Just because you trust a person doesn't mean that person trusts you. Mutuality is a dance, with each person tiptoeing around to see how the other responds. When we experience someone's being there for us when we fall or share a fault, trust is established. When trust is lopsided, one or two people become vulnerable, but others won't, and MEA is never realized. If one person feels trust but another does not, trust is not mutual and therefore will diminish a group's accountability factor.

Personal familiarity refers to how well you know a certain person. Like onions, people possess numerous layers in their personage. Depending on temperament, culture, and past hurts, these layers vary in thickness. Familiarity increases significantly when we experience people in a variety of situations, not just gathering together in a consistent environment such as Bible study or Sunday church. Until I see how you treat your family, deal with strangers, interact with work colleagues, handle pet peeves, and function in your house and work environments, I can't say I really know you. When we're unfamiliar with people, they can fool us, presenting their best side only and appearing better than they really are. You have no reason to believe otherwise, even when they appear preoccupied and not themselves.

How many times have you asked someone, "How are you doing?"

The person smiles and says, "Fine."

But when you know someone well, share trust, and have emotional investment, you can very naturally push back and respond, "Hey, Ben. You don't seem yourself today. What's up?"

Someone suggested that perhaps the greatest proof to the divinity of Jesus was that he basically went on a three-year camping trip with his learners and at the end, they still thought he was the Son of God. Typical church methods allow us to compartmentalize our faith, so that people only see us in limited settings. Others know us based on what we share in guarded moments, as opposed to observing us in a variety of circumstances.

When these three elements synergize in a relationship, you have Mutually Earned Accountability, the sweet spot resulting in the level and type of accountability that is most apt to be received and implemented. When we see Jesus telling his disciples that they lacked faith (Matt. 8:23–26; John 20:26–27), were lazy (Matt. 26:36–40), and even satanic (Matt. 16:22–23), it seems insensitive and abrupt. But the fact that the Twelve remained intact, except for one at the very end, shows that Jesus had earned the right to speak into their lives. They were convinced of his love, his character, and his commitment to them. He demonstrated this by sticking up for them (Mark 7:5–15), affirming their growth (Matt. 16:15–17), allowing them to join him in big events (John 6:1–15; 12:1–11), and believing in them enough to send them out to do his work (Matt. 28:18–22).

Selecting Your Travel Team Members

The purpose of a Travel Team is not to merely talk about God, but rather to do life together with an agreed agenda to include a spiritual emphasis, weaving it in and out of conversations, activities, and study. You're doing this for your soul. It's not Sunday school with socializing on the side. It's more like a casserole than meat, potato, and veggies à la carte. The typical methods of spiritual growth conditions us to compartmentalize our faith, disconnecting the spiritual from whole life involvement with God.

There is no cookie-cutter approach to establishing a Travel Team, but begin with chemistry. You should have a level of likeability among the three to ten others with whom you want to do life. But don't seek clones of yourself. The power of multiple, varying perspectives, along with the occasional friction and differences of opinions, are important to the growth process. Jesus's followers had some tense moments between them. This is not just a band of buddies, enjoying life together. While you're apt to develop some of the deepest and most meaningful relationships possible, there will be moments of conflict, irritation, and even frustration, which is another reason why people avoid such intimate, vulnerable relationships.

Begin by making a list of people you know. Try not to prejudge whether or not someone is interested in a deeper connection with God. Ask them. My experience tells me you may be surprised by who enlists. They may be from your work, neighborhood, church, or social networks. Chances are you'll be the glue for these people, so they may or may not have an instant affinity for each other. If you enjoy them, chances are they'll grow to like each other. You may want to make up a name for this group or create an excuse to hang out together socially, to discuss life or work, or to read a personal growth book for discussion. If possible, test the chemistry first and foster some familiarity. Don't start with a covenant.

Jesus told a parable about soils (Matt. 13:1–9), describing growth environments of four seeds. Only one grew and multiplied, because of its setting. Think of this Travel Team as your soul garden, the incubator for growth. You'll want to do as much as you can to hand select who is in the group, much like Jesus did. Where do you start? As we mentioned earlier, chances are slim that you'll be invited to be in another person's Travel Team, simply because so few people utilize Jesus's method. Since a Travel Team is different from most small groups, Bible studies, and friend circles, you may be able to use one of these existing groups that you can ratchet up to the Travel Team level in order to create Mutually Earned Accountability.

You may want to begin by making a list of potential people, which will require you to consider the type of Team you'd like to establish. As you look at the degrees of accountability, you'll likely want to go through Levels 1 and 2 before you raise the level of commitment. There will come a time when you'll want to intentionally see if people are ready for a deeper commitment. This is not a quantity issue as much as a quality issue, but typically, if your group meets biweekly, you'll want three to six months to bond and develop trust before you broach the subject. This is more of an organic process, not artificial or contrived. Yet it is intentional, just as a farmer intentionally plants a crop. If you are already in a group with Level 2 accountability, then you may be ready to pop the question, "Hey, I've been reading this book on spiritual intelligence. What would you think about going through this together to see if we'd like to take our group to the next level?"

Those who are in a church will often find a Travel Team consisting of people in their faith community most effective. The reason is that in addition to Travel Team activities, you'll likely be involved in other aspects of your faith community, such as worship services, retreats, and local and distant service projects. The downside of many parachurch organizations that gather people in small groups is that they tend to be disconnected from faith communities and create yet another department in an overly disjointed lifestyle. The benefit of Jesus's day was that most small villages were local and people felt connected. You'd wash your clothes with your neighbors, buy food from your friend, and help raise each others' kids. This lifestyle lent itself to the way Jesus grew souls. Today, we must intentionally strive to create a similar soul garden, but the local church or parish is the closest thing to this lost communal lifestyle.

One of the biggest challenges is often logistics. Finding times together in people's busy schedules is not easy, especially if your Travel Team has people with small kids, business professionals who travel, or single parents with work and childcare issues. This is not an optional "make it if you can" sort of gathering. Sometimes, you'll have Travel Team candidates who seem perfect, but they just aren't available. Commitment usually comes down to a matter of want and availability. The biggest challenge I've found is selling the commitment before people have experienced the benefits. That's why you may want to take it in stages. For example, you might begin meeting once a month for six months and then see how it goes. If people see an "exit" not far ahead, it's often easier for them to say "yes." Once you have a good Travel Team functioning, you can ask these people to tell their stories of what they've gotten out of their experience. Then you can increase the frequency and commitment.

Another common issue is whether to make a Travel Team coed or the same gender. There are pros and cons of each. One positive aspect of a coed group is that husbands and wives can participate together, helping each other be more accountable at home and beyond, and it is sometimes easier to find commitment when you're not proposing one more activity away from the spouse. Plus, there's a certain chemistry that changes in mixed groups, in that you'll gain gender perspectives and it feels more like life in general, where men and women interact.

Yet, as a general rule, this chemistry sometimes prevents people from sharing at a level that they might otherwise. For example, lust and pornography are common male issues that will likely be discussed in an all-male group, as trust grows and conversations go there. But having women present will likely keep men from sharing openly about these struggles. Actually, online pornography is also becoming a women's issue, and addressing that among men would be awkward. Sometimes a person's hesitancy to share deeply or candidly is a marital issue, where a husband or wife will not be open because of what is going on in the marriage.

Also in a coed group, there is the risk of emotional bonding with a person of the opposite sex, because you'll eventually get to places of deep sharing and serving others that add a chemical reaction which could distract from the group and may even become a negative temptation. One way to circumvent this liability is to schedule separate discussion times—men with men, women with women—during the more personal sharing.

In our experience, the cons of mixed groups tend to outweigh the pros. The exception is when the Path Finder is experienced and the participants have a good level of emotional intelligence. And sometimes mixed groups are easier sells, because a single group satisfies a vital social component without adding more time out of one's schedule.

We are all in favor of mixed-gender groups, whether they are larger fellowships, less committed social groups, or even occasional date nights that include Travel Team member spouses or even combining Travel Teams for service projects. But generally, same-gender Travel Teams or consistent divided discussion times and outings enhance growth and depth of discussion.

Our gender differences are significant enough that separating makes the most sense. The best scenario is if you have a

Travel Team of men and a Travel Team of women who do some of the experiential elements together, which we'll discuss later. This adds a degree of complication to the Travel Team, but it can also serve to enhance the total experience and make the commitment easier for those who want to participate as spouses.

The Invitation

As I mentioned, a natural way to get people to consider a Travel Team is by reading this book together and discussing the ideas. The simple process of interacting with the concepts is a means of drawing a line in the sand to see who may and may not be ready for such a commitment. You may simply try explaining the principles you're learning, sharing them with your fellow group members. It may come down to leaving an existing group to afford you more time to begin one with the goal of soul growth via these methods.

You may want to begin from scratch, if you're like the majority of people who are not in any existing type of spiritually oriented group or you'd like to start fresh. Chances are that you have people in your sphere of influence who would be willing to journey with you in a group like this. A fundamental of human nature is a yearning to belong. Although we desire intimacy, we pursue anonymity, which leaves us lonely and unsupported. We long to be both understood and accepted. Combine this hunger for a circle of friends with spiritual interest, and you will likely be surprised by who'll be open to participating. Don't necessarily pursue religious types. Many in this psychographic want a place to preach, lecture, or sell their doctrinal agenda. Jesus didn't shop the religious schools for his disciples. He hung around the fish docks, village markets, and even the local IRS office (Matthew).

My wife and I began a couples group a few months after moving to the Monterey, California, area. We began with a list of people that Nancy had met from her staff role at the church. We looked at the calendar, set a date, and then phoned people. A few had expressed interest in being in a couples group and a few had no idea why we were calling. "We're putting together a potluck dinner a few Sundays from now, meeting from 5:30–7:30 p.m., to see who might be interested in participating in a couples group. This is a one-time commitment. We're just testing the water." A little over half of the people were available and/or interested.

During the social, we ate, shared names and brief introductions of our families, and then I introduced the idea for a different kind of group. We decided to begin biweekly due to our lifestyles and take the first ninety days simply to get to know each other and see if there was a good chemistry for us. We could invite others during that time, but after that, we would see who wanted to go forward and who did not. The next time commitment was for six months, to go further in and then see who wanted to re-up. We called our Travel Team a Journey Group and acknowledged the four components, clarifying that this was not a Bible study per se or just a social group.

Logistic Ideas

Select a location for your regular Travel Team meetings that is relatively free from distractions such as phones, children, other people, and noise. That is why restaurants and cafés rarely work for the typical gathering venue.

Years of experimenting with a variety of formats has taught me that the most effective schedule is weekly, but the growing time pressures in our culture make biweekly meetings preferred by many, especially during the first six to nine months. A less than weekly schedule can create emotional distance in members who miss a meeting, not to mention the challenge of remembering the rotation.

Meeting lengths of one to two hours are best. Women typically prefer longer; men shorter. Meetings shorter than one hour usually do not get to a level of sufficient sharing or allow for a balanced meeting that includes Directions, prayer, discussion, and friendly conversation. Rushing the agenda detracts from the chemistry of the group. But remember, this is not just a classroom/living room/office format. You'll be doing real-world activities that will be described more fully in chapter six.

In most communities, the school year works better for scheduling than the calendar year. Less than six months is often too short for a group to bond well and does not allow as much time to let life flow through the Travel Team, limiting the experiences shared. While groups that bond may want to meet longer than nine to twelve months, our recommendation is to modify the format so that the Travel Team members begin to experience more service and leadership roles. Some may want to take the group even deeper, while others go lighter for accountability. The goal of the Travel Team is not to become an exclusive clique but to produce people who can reproduce themselves into the lives of others.

Establishing a Strong, Clear Covenant

While it seems legalistic, a written Travel Team covenant can be a good communication tool as well as a means to heighten the awareness that members are committed to each other in community. The Path Finder can provide a basic, recommended template, but participants should have an opportunity to give input in order to increase ownership for the agreement. Providing a finished, written document that is signed by everyone can serve as a ceremonial event to seal the group. Make sure participants retain a copy, in case you have to refer to it later for accountability. These individuals are now partners in life, resulting in growth and SI.

Sample of a Written Travel Team Covenant

Because we believe that soul growth in community is an effective means of spiritual development, we agree to both give and receive accountability to the following items:

1. I will do my best to make our meeting times punctually. If I cannot attend due to sickness or travel, I will inform my partner in advance if at all possible.
2. If I cannot make a meeting, it is my responsibility to find out what we discussed and catch up on any assignments that may have been given at the meeting. If my partner is gone, I will do my best to contact him and update him on meeting themes and assignments.
3. I will come to meetings ready to participate, with any assignments completed to the best of my ability.
4. I agree to encourage other group members, provide support for them during difficult times, and pray for them on a consistent basis.
5. Because participation is vital, I understand that if I miss more than three meetings, I voluntarily submit my resignation, so as not to decrease the experience of others by my unwillingness or inability to commit to this group.
6. I agree that everything that is shared within our group meetings is to be held in strict confidence, unless specific permission is granted otherwise.
7. I agree to participate in our planned service activities to the best of my ability, understanding that this is an important part of our unity as a group and growth as an individual.

I realize that my membership in this group is based on my adherence to the above covenantal elements.
I will keep these agreements to the best of my ability through
_____ (date)

Signed _____
date _____
(One copy goes to the participant and one to the navigator/Path Finder.)

Determining a Schedule

Choosing Directions resources, study topics, and reading expectations, as well as sharing LifeLines, is a good way to begin. Schedule one or two socials that are just for fun, followed by a periodic service activity that you do as a Travel Team. One of the socials might be good to do as couples or families if participants are married. Seeing people interact with their family members gives other participants a better feel of what each person is like. Discuss and schedule one or two service activities, such as serving the homeless or a half-day mission event. One of the most effective Travel Team events is an overnight retreat. Getting away from home for at least twenty-four hours provides unique learning and bonding experiences, unavailable in short, formal settings.

A functional ninety-minute meeting format might include:

Ten minutes for shooting the breeze/getting settled/ refreshments

Twenty minutes for more intentional group sharing, "checking in" with each other

Forty minutes for Directions (Bible study, video lesson, etc.) and discussion

Twenty minutes for prayer/wrap-up discussion/service event planning/good-byes

Implementing a Covenant

The covenant is an agreement that carries power, as long as it is implemented. When Travel Team participants begin to falter in attendance, preparation, or other elements spelled out in the agreement, it is the Path Finder's responsibility to raise the issue. A one-on-one conversation may be sufficient, but there may also come a time for group discussion. When a participant is haphazard in commitment, it is better to let the member go than to diminish his or her idea of what a Travel Team is, as well as for the sake of the other members. The benefit of a formal covenant is that members basically submit their own resignations when they fail to keep the predetermined agreements, taking the negative edge away from the Path Finder and other participants when Mutually Earned Accountability needs to be demonstrated to a wandering member. Because each member is vital to the team's effectiveness, the group needs to decide on an appropriate response. While grace is vital, accountability is also important. The Travel Team needs to discuss how the group is functioning, which may include how individuals are impacting each other positively and negatively. While we'll not go into small group dynamics at this point, a savvy Path Finder/navigator will prayerfully consider a loving but healthy discussion.

Practical Questions and Answers

What if someone quits?

Losing a Travel Team member impacts everyone. If someone does not bond in the beginning, it is less of an issue. But when someone drops out in the middle or near the end, there is often a sense of disappointment among the others. Address this and have the group discuss their feelings, frustrations, thoughts, and appropriate responses. If several people drop out, you might consider causes, such as a lack of clarity of expectations in the beginning, and/or the ability of the Path Finder. You may decide to regroup with new team members.

What if someone strays spiritually?

If a person goes through a personal time of temptation and failure, pulling away from God, and/or struggles with a personal issue that makes him or her withdraw, it is the team's responsibility to reach out. A Travel Team is hypocritical if it does not extend a hand to a member who is flailing, spiritually or otherwise. The big decision is how members go about this. Discuss options with honor and respect in mind and then act on the best option(s).

What do you study? How do you select effective Direction resources?

The power of a Travel Team is not in the curriculum, but the community. There are a plethora of resources available these days. You can initially gather a group around a common interest and let friendships take it to the next step. You can also survey participants as to what they would like to read or study. Topical Bible studies, a book discussion, and any number of combinations are viable. Many resources do not require significant Bible knowledge or navigator preparation. Asking others for recommendations and/or perusing a large Christian bookstore are good ways to find resource materials.

How long do you continue a Travel Team?

After a team has met for nine to twelve months, you may find it time to end or re-up. Some teams begin to lose energy toward the end of their commitments. Addressing this is the responsibility of the Path Finder/navigator, without any sense of failure. Energy flows up and down in Travel Teams as in any group. Try to end before all the energy has left the group. You may want to rewrite the covenant so that it continues to serve the participants. When a group outgrows its initial agreement, this is a good challenge. The positive influence of a bonded team is that friendships provide for lifelong memories and growth. The negative of a bonded team is that without knowing, it can become ingrown, exclusive, and unhealthy. Gaining input from a more experienced Path Finder outside of your group may be helpful in terms of determining length, ebb, and flow. This is less of a problem when the Travel Team remains focused on periodically Experiencing the Trip through service projects and interacting with others.

What do you do when a team member misses a meeting?

One way to make sure a person feels as though they've not fully missed out on a meeting is to assign partners. The responsibility of a partner is to let the other one know when he or she cannot make a meeting, so that the group is not wondering. The other responsibility is for the attending part-ner to make contact with his or her absent partner before the next meeting in order to share topics, lesson materials, and update the person as to what happened. This takes the load of follow-up off the shoulders of the navigator.

Five Common Reasons Travel Teams Don't Gel

All teams have life spans and most groups run into a few snags taking off or continuing well. Even Jesus had his challenges (e.g., Judas). Persevere, but be aware of the most common Travel Team snags.

1. *Failure to establish a reasonable covenant.* While you do not need a written document, there should be clarity as to expectations, requirements, and participation levels. When agreement issues are vague or unreasonable, the group is doomed to have problems.

2. *Failure of Path Finder/navigator to carry out the cov-enant and hold members accountable.* Shepherding a Travel Team is an art, but much of the power comes in terms of follow-through and Mutually Earned Ac-countability. That tends to be a responsibility of the Path Finder.

3. *Lack of participation among members/dropping out.* You cannot force adult learners to comply. If a per-son shows up late, misses meetings, fails to follow up, and participates poorly by dominating conversation or preaching, the Path Finder/navigator must lovingly confront the situation. This preserves a healthy environ-ment for the other participants.

4. *Too much time shooting the breeze.* Every group is dif-ferent in terms of personality types and task/people orientation. The navigator needs to help the group re-main on the schedule that was outlined in the covenant.

84

Ask members individually or as a group for feedback on how the meetings are functioning.

5. *Classroom-only experiences*. Avoiding outside trips, projects, and events often limits the health of a team as we noted in the discussion of SI methods. By procrastinating on the planning of service projects and overnight retreats, you ignore the power of experiential learning.

Keep in mind that the Travel Team is just one of four essential parts leading to spiritual intelligence, but it is the most important one for beginning. Think of it as the pot and soil for a plant, or the canvas for a painting, or the vehicle for a trip. This group not only makes the journey more enjoyable, it makes it possible.

Interaction Ideas:

1. Why do you think Jesus spent so much time with so few people, when his time was limited and the needs were so great?

2. Why do you think we typically emphasize other aspects of spiritual growth rather than developing a good Travel Team (e.g., events, large group services, lower commitment small groups)?

3. Share a story of a time when you were or were not effectively accountable.

4. Make a short list of people right now who you think might be candidates for your Travel Team.

5. If it seems appropriate, brainstorm some initial kickoff ideas.

Activity: Get a box of one hundred metal paper clips for every three to four people in your group. Dump them in a pile. The assignment is for each person to make a chain with as many individual clips as he or she can in thirty seconds. Add the totals and divide by the number of people to determine an average. Then, do this again with everyone working on a single chain together. Only individual clips can be used. You may want to plan a strategy before starting. Count the total. How does this compare with the average of the individual chains? How is this like pursuing spiritual growth with a team of people?

FIVE

Directions

GPS for the Soul

My college buddy Mark Dill and I were speaking at a church in West Virginia the week before our college commencement ceremony. After the Sunday evening service, we hopped in the car to drive through the night toward Kankakee, Illinois, an hour south of Chicago. Unfortunately, the directions we had weren't very accurate. We found ourselves driving around in circles in the back roads of West Virginia. We stopped to clarify our location and got more bad advice, losing precious time. We were about to miss our own graduation, disappointing our families who had traveled to attend. Finally, one-half hour before "Pomp and Circumstance" began, we pulled into our dorm parking lot and donned our robes and mortar boards, dead tired.

We've all experienced bad directions and flawed maps. That's why it's so important to get good advice on journeys. A second element of Jesus's method for growing souls is Directions. A Travel Team without Directions is little more than a wandering mob. Jesus received Directions and he also gave Directions to his learners.

When you're on a long trip, having a map is important. In ancient times, this consisted of stars and simple markers along the path. More formal signage evolved, some noting distances. Cartographers began recording locations on parchment. Modern technology now provides computer-generated mapping such as MapQuest and handheld as well as automotive GPS systems that tell us where to turn. But the basics remain the same. Directions are needed when you're on any journey of significance. Wandering wastes precious time and can ultimately take you where you don't want to go.

We frequently see Directions interrelated with Jesus. Prophecies, angels, and a star pointed to his birth. Before beginning his public ministry, the Spirit led Jesus to be tested in the desert (Matt. 4:1–11). We see him seeking Directions numerous times in the form of prayer and meditation (Mark 1:35–39; John 17).

Jesus was also adept at finding Directions in holy writings. As a preteen, he interacted with religious teachers in the temple. Several times throughout his ministry, he referred to Directions from Old Testament Scriptures (Matt. 5:38; Mark 4:12; Luke 10:27), even quoting them as he died (Matt. 27:46).

Jesus's learners received quite a few Directions from him on their journey. There were hillside speeches, parables along the road, and kingdom comments here and there during teachable moments. Even today, Jesus's words serve as Directions, giving his followers guidance for living, understanding of the spiritual realm, and insight regarding what is needed to know God.

These are reliable Directions, far more dependable than so much advice from others:

"Oh yes, you oughta divorce the bum. He's a jerk. Get on with life."

"You should take the job and just see what happens."

"Dreaming is for rich people. You've got to pay the bills. Everything in moderation. That's what my father taught me."

Opinions are a dime a dozen. No matter how many people offer their thoughts, we need more reliable Directions.

Directions Sources

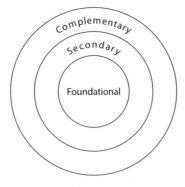

Directions can come from a variety of sources, but we're best off when they are based on or complement reliable ones.

Foundational: Focusing on Jesus's teachings, life events, and the writings he relied on (the Old Testament) are essential for SI. In the past, a seminary or Bible college degree was needed to use the tools provided by scholars, but today there are numerous versions of the Bible and user-friendly resources (e.g., www.biblegateway.com) you can access to develop your soul. "I gain understanding from your precepts; therefore I hate every wrong path. Your word is a lamp to my feet and a light for my path" (Ps. 119:104–5).

Secondary: These sources are based on Scripture, varying in depth and weight. Examples of these include sermons and Bible studies. These are often written and delivered by people who have studied Scripture and done some of the foundational work for you. But realize such writings and talks are biased by the worldviews, experiences, and doctrinal belief systems of the authors. These do not make them wrong, but be aware there's a difference between what someone says a passage teaches and what it actually meant in the context in which it was given. Half a dozen earnest, trained individuals can look at a single passage and make different inferences from the same source, each believing his or hers more correct than the others.

Less foundational secondary sources tend to be topical sermons (applying a variety of Scriptures to a topic), gospel music, and any number of books that include Scriptures in varying proportions. Prayer, meditation, and counsel from people who sense God's interaction in your life are secondary means of gaining Directions. Dependability increases as they find support in foundational sources.

Complementary: Many people overlook inspiring and powerful ways that God provides Directions through means that have no direct correlation to holy writings. This may include books on personal growth and improvement (e.g., *The Seven Habits of Highly Successful People, The Greatest Miracle in the World*), music (e.g., U2, Celtic instrumental), poetry (e.g., Thoreau, Frost, Milton), nature (e.g., parks, mountains, oceans, rivers), television programs (e.g., "Touched by an Angel," "Extreme Makeover: Home Edition"), and movies. I've found spiritual Directions from films such as *Ghandi, Patch Adams, Somewhere in Time, Star Wars, Braveheart, The Matrix,* and *The Bucket List*. None of these is religious in nature or necessarily Christian. But when you are open to God providing Direction from a number of sources, you'll often be surprised by the means he uses. The arts can unlock spiritual insights in both spectator and participant.

One of the most impactful books in my life was a little, inspirational title by Og Mandino, *The Greatest Miracle in the World*. When I began reading it, I couldn't put it down. Even though it's not a Christian book per se, God used it powerfully to speak into my life. The book concludes with a letter supposedly from God to the main character in the book. While it was the product of a contemporary writer, it complemented so much of what I'd been taught in church, but for whatever reason had never been able to grasp emotionally. I sobbed uncontrollably as I read it. I read it over and over, perhaps half a dozen times.

The key word is "complementary," meaning these are not your sole means of finding Directions. They should complement and not contradict foundational sources. People using complementary sources solely or even primarily for their Directions are easily detoured from understanding truths that can catalyze the growth we are speaking of in spiritual intelligence. At the same time, people who rely only on foundational and secondary sources fail to see truths that God brings through a variety of means on a larger scale, thus limiting their maturation.

God used mountains, streams, trees, babies, sheep, and desert to inspire the Psalm writers. For others in the Bible, it was fish, a whale, fire, wind, and even a donkey. We must not sequester God to a certain setting or specific time, such as when someone is speaking about God or people are reading the Bible. Holy Scriptures were quite often the result of God using circumstances, people, and natural means to convey Directions. Yet we overlook the method God used, looking only at the results of this method (namely, the Scriptures themselves) and ignoring what God might be saying through our surroundings. But God uses the same method today, showing us Directions from everyday inspirations in addition to holy writings.

Prayer, Meditation, and Journaling

Scores believe that Jesus was the son of God, sharing DNA with the Creator of the universe. Yet Jesus continually went to God for guidance and strength. One morning, Jesus arose early in the morning to go up the mountain to pray (Mark 1:35). When he came down, the disciples frantically asked where he'd been, informing him that there were people waiting to see him. But because of the Directions he'd received that morning, Jesus knew he needed to be moving on to the next village. He told them, "Let's go."

A very important part of Directions involves prayer and meditation. This is akin to preparing the soil in a garden so it can absorb moisture, fertilizer, and air. Followers of Jesus believe that God hears and answers prayers and is directly involved with the person praying, not just the prayers themselves. The latter is where the typical approach to these practices falls short. As in the SI journey, the implementation of these actions preps our souls for growth.

A few weeks ago, I was wrestling with feelings of discouragement. I closed my laptop, walked down the street from the coffee shop where I was writing, and just sat on a log, overlooking beautiful Carmel Beach. The waves lapped on the shores and the sun shone through partly cloudy skies. Not more than ten minutes into my time alone with God, I felt an amazing sense of encouragement and hope. There were no Scriptures, sermons, worship songs, or Christian living books, but the combination of nature's beauty and a heart yearning for God provided what I needed at the moment. God moments like these are all around us, if we're willing to seek them.

One of the best sources of soul stimulation is the ageless tradition of writing our thoughts and prayers. As a writer, I have come to realize how the practice helps us remain focused as we articulate our thoughts. Our brains operate at a different level as we formulate ideas into words. There is the added benefit of kinesthetic learning. The sheer physical activity required to write increases retention because it forces the brain to operate at another level in a different area. The downside of journaling, whether by pen or computer, is that it can be distracting for those who end up focusing on spelling and grammar. The best advice is to learn a few methods, such as formal letter writing or journalistic note taking. Use one or more as seems fitting. We would not have the holy writings today were it not for people who journaled their experiences.

If I'm honest with myself, sometimes I don't do these disciplines simply because I'm lazy, much the same as when I don't balance my checkbook, exercise, say no to a second helping of dessert, or clear my office of paper stacks. But confessing these shortcomings to my Travel Team lessens the internal guilt and feeling of defeat and heightens the chance I'll do the discipline, especially if it becomes a group assignment.

Individual and Travel Team praying are important practices. Listening for God and reporting God sightings is an effective way to open our senses to spiritual activity in our daily lives. Sure, there will be those who claim to hear God tell them what shirt to wear or that the leaf blowing across the sidewalk was a sign to quit their job, but don't let those with overactive imaginations prevent you from authentically sensing God interacting with you through circumstances, thoughts, and comments from others.

Just as you cannot see or touch the electrical waves that your cell phone and satellite television pick up, you cannot see or touch God's conveying Directions to you, though he desires to do just that. Prayer is little more than turning on your system and aiming your satellite dish toward the source of the signal. Directions come to us through cognitive and intuitive means. Listening to a sermon or lesson and reading Scripture or a book tend to be cognitive and left-brained activities. When combined with singing, listening to music, praying, journaling, and being quiet before God—right-brained activities—we incorporate both dimensions of our mind in spiritual pursuit. One without the other will not yield the same results.

Getting Directions

Good Directions can come to you through a variety of means. You can simply open the Bible and begin reading and meditating on it yourself or jot down ideas and questions about what you read. Some people rely fully on a sermon they receive from a television preacher, local church pastor, or priest's homily. This can be good if it is discussed in the context of a Travel Team, but has significantly less impact otherwise. Exceptions exist, but the typical person has lost 90 percent of the message before he or she leaves the service, and another 90 percent of what remains within seventy-two hours. If you ask most people what the last sermon they heard was about, most will not be able to tell you, in spite of nearly twenty-five hours per week the typical pastor invests in sermon preparation and delivery. A little math shows that if three hundred thousand churches present, at one each, three hundred thousand weekly messages, paying the pastor an average salary of $40,000 per year, we spend $6 billion per year and just over $115 million per week in sermon preparation and delivery in the United States alone.

Having prepared and delivered nearly one thousand messages myself, I am not one to throw stones at pastors, even though I've experienced a boatload of boring ones. But even mediocre messages can provide life-changing Directions *if* used properly. The problem is that even fantastic teaching typically lies dormant because we rely on the method of broadcast and inspiration, instead of narrowcasting and application. Preaching to the masses is akin to a farmer's flinging seed on the ground, yielding limited returns because of the unreceptive soils. But Jesus targeted his messages to the Twelve because they were few and he knew them well. This is the potency of providing Directions for a Travel Team.

If we're pretty much on our own for our soul's growth, how do we use the plethora of Directions available through sermons, Bible studies, books, podcasts, CDs, and DVDs? Hearing a generic talk or reading a study prepared for the masses is rarely sufficient to move Directions beyond an intellectual level. You cannot presume other people know what it is you need, at least not on an individual basis. You'll probably need to pick and choose, as you do with shopping, eating out, exercising, and surfing the Internet.

One of my favorite writing settings is Panera Bread, a national chain of homey cafés that provide breads, food, coffee, and my favorite amenity, free WiFi. The other day I was sitting in a Panera, and I saw a businessman with a banana from home and a Starbucks coffee cup, who ordered a Panera bagel. I looked over at a college student who'd brought his own juice in a plastic bottle to go with his Panera bagel. In the same room, a woman had a Panera coffee and bagel, but sliced tomatoes she'd brought in a plastic baggie along with cream cheese from a jar that she pulled from her purse. While I doubt Panera smiles on the practice of people bringing their own food, people do, in order to augment their budget or taste. I can't count how many times my family has brought a McDonald's bag into a different restaurant because at least one of the boys didn't care for Mom's or Dad's choice of eating establishment.

As you grow your soul, you'll want to intentionally select the content as well as implement it effectively. If you want to obtain SI, you cannot randomly show up for church, turn on your favorite religious broadcaster, or haphazardly open your Bible, running your finger down the page. The problem is primarily methodological, not informational.

Goldilocks Directions

Finding Directions that are just right—not too hard and not too soft—is difficult. The problem is a combination of where you are in your journey and the type or style of Directions you're receiving. During graduate school I studied various therapy styles based on the different schools of thought. The big idea was that a client benefits from a specific style of therapy, based on his or her current needs. One single type is not likely to be effective the entire way.

I've noticed a pride among certain preachers and teachers who convey the idea that their style is best. I hear a similar sentiment from parishioners who brag about whose church they attend. Many eventually leave the congregation saying, "I'm looking for better preaching." Finding effective teaching is not easy, but realize that Directions alone are insufficient to obtain spiritual intelligence.

Churches that place a majority of their soul growth emphasis on teaching risk making the Bible an object of worship. The gospel existed before the Bible. Scriptures should be thought of as a revelation of God, aiding us in interacting with our Creator and discovering our purpose, but they do not contain everything we can experience from God.

Navigating with a Travel Team

How should a Travel Team find and discern Directions? There are a variety of ways for this to happen, but often there is a navigator on the Team, a person who is primarily responsible for keeping the Team on course. The navigator is not a dictator, making decisions while oblivious to the interests and opinions of the group. The navigator's primary responsibility is making sure that Directions are a part of the regular gathering time.

There is a plethora of user-friendly and effective resources available. Many find that a simple reading and discussion of the Bible is interesting, beginning at the start of one of the sixty-six books and moving through it. The navigator can prepare a lesson based on a particular passage, or the team can simply respond to a journalistic reporting technique, asking who, what, when, where, and why. Remember, the primary goal is not content analysis that results in academic dialogue. The goal is application. How is this going to change the way you view life, marriage, parenting, business, thoughts, attitudes, and priorities?

Other people prefer a topical approach that begins with a theme of interest and then uses the Bible as a means for gaining light on the topic. This is often an easier approach to initially create team interest. The weakness of this method is hopscotching around so that you lose the context of a passage. It is akin to cutting out sections of a newspaper story. The resulting collage may not reflect the original meaning because you lifted the themes away from their backgrounds that gave them meaning.

There are any number of books, Bible study resources, CDs, DVDs, and podcasts that can provide Directions for your Travel Team. If you want suggestions for finding a quality resource, you may want to ask your pastor or priest and then present these ideas to your Travel Team. Like laying out a map for a group of friends on a road trip, you'll want their input for your journey.

If all your members are a part of the same faith community, you might consider taking the pastor's or priest's weekend message as fodder for discussion and dialogue. The goal is not to critique it or give your opinion on whether you thought he or she was right, wrong, or somewhere in between. Rather, the objective is to consider what God might be trying to teach you through it and how you can begin to change the way you live as a result of this new insight.

Developing a Framework for Directions

The Bible is our main "map," above any other type of Direction, but it should not become the object of our faith as many seem to make it. The goal of a map is to lead us somewhere, to help us arrive, not to become the revered destination itself. Therefore, we want to see it as a tool for progressing in our journey. Since you are responsible for your own soul growth, you'll want to develop a draft or framework of how the Bible can be better understood and the teachings you receive better organized.

So how do you develop such a draft or framework? Any serious student has wrestled with that just-right balance of understanding teaching that is too light or too heavy, too shallow, or too deep. Most of us who've been around the church for a while have met those people who sink our ships with too much input, going into doctrinal detail that overwhelms us with information, if not boring us to death in the process. A little boy stood by his parents, looked up to the sky, and saw a plane flying overhead. He asked his mom, "How do planes fly?" The mother asked, "I'm just curious, why didn't you ask your dad?" The boy responded, "Because, I didn't want to know that much about it."

Nevertheless, biblical illiteracy is a growing concern, even among many people owning multiple Bibles and attending countless church services. The main reason for this ignorance may have less to do with the amount of information we're introduced to than it does the breadth and format of teaching. We've failed to create skills and structures with which to organize the many thoughts and truths we're presented with in any given service or study event. Most Sunday message themes lack big-picture planning. Add to that the hit-or-miss attendance of most people and you end up with sizable gaps in biblical Directions.

Over the years, my wife and I have had the joy of working with a number of people, both those who are very new to the ways of Jesus and those quite familiar with biblical Directions. Following is a list of four trilogies that we've found helpful in assisting people as they develop a biblical Directions foundation.

Three Knowledge Areas
1. *Big picture of the Bible*

- How did we get the Bible?
- How do the books work together as a whole?

98

- Why is the Bible considered to be the authoritative source on and about God?

2. Section overviews

- What are the historical, poetic/wisdom, prophetic, and letters/theology sections?
- What is the role of the Old and New Testaments?
- How do these sections differ and how are they similar to each other?

3. Book main themes

- What are the megathemes of each book?
- Who are the characters in or behind the scenes?
- How does this book fit into the big picture?

Three Content Categories

1. *Stories* (who, what, when, where, how, why)
Think of Bible stories as news clips of how people interact with each other and how God relates with and responds to people. Knowing the classic stories, main characters, and circumstances around these stories is an important part of gaining Bible knowledge and grasping their inherent truths.

2. *Principles* (truths, doctrines, theology)
Every story is told for a reason. What are the main principles and truths you can learn from them? In the more dense teaching passages, what do we learn about God, his character, how he responds to certain attitudes and actions, and his fundamental values?

3. *Applications* (then and now context, obedience)
None of the previous information creates significant life change if it is not applied. Making the connection from those

times to these times is crucial. How does this impact your life, priorities, actions, attitudes, and interactions with people? Application means translating concepts and others' experiences into your own world. This in turn requires changes in your life so that deeper issues of control, choice, and will are confronted. Without application, you've turned into a walking textbook who can parrot ideas, but who lacks life transformation.

Three Study Approaches

While there are numerous ways to approach the Bible, most can be placed within three basic categories. The ability to use any and all of these skills broadens your ability to discover quality Directions, empowering you to stop relying solely on professional teachers and theologians.

1. *Inductive:* neutral, natural investigation

This approach looks at a book, chapter, or passage for what it is, in and of itself. Our goal is to let the passage set the agenda for us as we study it. This helps us avoid loading the deck and lessens the risk of taking a passage out of context, which distorts the Directions. We do not try to read into the Scriptures or make them fit our assumptions. By letting the passage set the agenda, we strive to understand the people in the text, the historical and cultural context, what is going on and why, and what it means for us.

2. *Deductive:* topical, targets adult learning

This approach tends to be more popular because it begins with a specific question or problem and seeks a biblical perspective on the issue. You set the agenda. Adults tend to learn best when they perceive specific problems to solve. You may want to do a study on the Holy Spirit, marriage, parenting, stress, leadership, holiness, or any number of other topics. By using resource tools, you look at a variety of Bible passages that touch on these themes. By cross-referencing and doing topical studies, you perceive various angles on the same subject, which leads to application of the learned principles.

3. *Devotional:* inspiration, meditation, motivation

Everyone needs spiritual inspiration and motivation. By using the Bible as a tool for quiet time—less cognitive and more emotive—you strive to create an atmosphere for meditation and listening to God. Examples are using the Psalms as a prayer guide, focusing on Jesus's teachings for personal applications, and reading a Proverb for daily wisdom. A devotional approach to the Bible should not be your only one, but it certainly should be a primary style you incorporate during self-feeding and time alone with God.

Three Study Skills

Basic study skills provide a disciple with a range of abilities to foster soul growth, check out the reliability of teachers, and provide tools as a Path Finder. Here are three skill areas that are important for the disciple.

1. *Study tools*

Unlike in the past, we now have the opportunity to possess some of the finest scholarly resources available. Commentaries, concordances, Bible atlases, dictionaries, and encyclopedias, all driven by powerful computer search engines, allow common people uncommon knowledge. The Internet has a growing number of services available for fast research. As you can imagine, the downside of this technology is that a lot of mediocre and spiritually toxic ideas are promoted. The primary limitations today are no longer money and availability, but sparse training as to what these resources are and how they can be used.

2. *Self-feeding know-how*

When children are babies, we bottle- or spoon-feed them, but when they get older, they learn to feed themselves. When people have a learning or physical disability, we have to continue to feed them, even when they would be old enough to do this if they were healthy. In similar fashion, when you become spiritually mature, you should be comfortable and competent to feed yourself soul food. The goal is not to do this in order to avoid small group fellowship and corporate worship, but rather to bring into these events a heart that is growing, vibrant, and ready to worship and serve. Relying on another for your spiritual food is unnecessary. You need to feed every day, not just sporadically as your schedule allows someone else to prepare your food. Devotions, quiet time, prayer, personal study, and meditation are all formats for this.

3. Investigative skills

What do you do if someone asks you a question about the Bible or God? Do you shrug your shoulders and say, "I dunno"? Or do you respond, "That's a good question. Give me a couple days to do some research, and I'll get back to you"? Knowing how to do your own Bible study, using available tools and tapping scholarly input, is essential for any learner. Instead of relying on "Let me call my pastor" as a response, you can defend your faith, base it on Scriptures, and explain the basis for fundamental Christian beliefs. Just because an idea is in print, or is taught by a well-known preacher or talk-show host, or is in a popular book, does not make it right. How do you know if it's right? With a little practice, you can go find a passage and support or refute something that seems logical or is controversial. By avoiding dependence on others, we enhance our ability to grow and apply more truth.

A Word of Caution

Finding your Directions from quality sources is important. Begin with the Bible and work out from there. History is full of people making outlandish statements based on their interpretation of Scripture, so be wary of those claiming authority. Don't be cynical, but also don't be naive.

Remember, knowledge of Scriptures alone does not result in SI. Some of the most educated people in Jesus's day were among the most deceived, assuming their education was equal to maturation. Jesus said,

> Woe to you, teachers of the law and Pharisees, you hypocrites! You are like whitewashed tombs, which look beautiful on the outside, but on the inside are full of dead men's bones and everything unclean. In the same way, on the outside you appear to people as righteous but on the inside you are full of hypocrisy and wickedness. (Matt. 23:27–28)

Jesus taught his learners:

> A farmer went out to sow his seed. As he was scattering the seed, some fell along the path, and the birds came and ate it up. Some fell on rocky places, where it did not have much soil. It sprang up quickly, because the soil was shallow. But when the sun came up, the plants were scorched, and they withered because they had no root. Other seed fell among thorns, which grew up and choked the plants. Still other seed fell on good soil, where it produced a crop—a hundred, sixty or thirty times what was sown. (Matt. 13:3–8)

If the seed is the Direction, the soil represents the receptivity of your soul.

Some people see results because of their spiritual intelligence, their readiness to receive and respond to truth. Jesus explained it this way, "But the one who received the seed that fell on good soil is the man who hears the word and understands it. He produces a crop, yielding a hundred, sixty or thirty times what was sown" (Matt. 13:23). The factor determining growth is understanding and application versus hearing alone. Some suggest that if people merely hear good

Directions, they cannot object to the irresistible nature of the message. I have seen growth from this method, but not maturity. Jesus said, "My mother and brothers are those who hear God's word and *put it into practice*" (Luke 8:21; emphasis mine). Again he said, "Blessed rather are those who hear the word of God and *obey it*" (Luke 11:28; emphasis mine). Without the three other SI methods, Directions seduce us into believing we've arrived when in reality we've just gotten on the plane.

> Therefore, get rid of all moral filth and the evil that is so prevalent and humbly accept the word planted in you, which can save you. *Do not merely listen to the word, and so deceive yourselves*. Do what it says. Anyone who listens to the word but does not do what it says is like a man who looks at his face in a mirror and, after looking at himself, goes away and immediately forgets what he looks like. But the man who looks intently into the perfect law that gives freedom, and continues to do this, not forgetting what he has heard, but doing it—he will be blessed in what he does. If anyone considers himself religious and yet does not keep a tight rein on his tongue, he deceives himself and his religion is worthless. Religion that God our Father accepts as pure and faultless is this: to look after orphans and widows in their distress and to keep oneself from being polluted by the world. (James 1:21–27; emphasis mine)

Deception results from thinking that once we've heard Directions, we've applied them. Jesus said, "You diligently study the Scriptures because you think that by them you possess eternal life. These are the Scriptures that testify about me, yet you refuse to come to me to have life" (John 5:39–40).

There are two primary words for *knowing* in the Bible. One refers to knowing intellectually, academically. "I know candy bars are sweet, because the contents say they contain sugar and because people tell me they are." The other has to do with experiential knowing. "I know candy bars are sweet, because I've tasted them." Knowing about God and knowing God personally are different matters, though they are designed to be complementary. An important part of obtaining SI is getting good Directions and using them in harmony with the other methods Jesus used.

Interaction Ideas:

1. What is one thing you got out of this chapter?

2. What are the pros and cons of considering Directions beyond the Bible?

3. The author states that some people seem to make the map their destination. What do you think about that and why?

4. How would you like to improve your pursuit of reliable Directions?

Activity: If possible, select a destination within a half hour drive that members in your group will not recognize. Place the following info in envelopes and divide the group into three vehicles. One receives the address alone, one the address with a map or directions, and one with a GPS device. After you get to the location, talk about the differences in directions and their results. Discuss how this relates to spiritual Directions.

SIX

Experiencing the Trip

Activating Your Passion and Knowledge

For the most part, Jesus avoided the monologue method of education, also known as death by lecture. He told stories and led
learners. He gave them tasks to accomplish; asked them questions; let them talk, ask, argue, and debate. Sometimes Jesus
interrupted conversations to challenge them. He made mud to
heal a blind man, instructed the learners to find tax money in
the mouth of a fish, washed the disciples' feet, and transformed
a Passover meal into one of the most revered, multisensory
experiences still in use today (communion/Eucharist).

The typical seminarian focuses on what Jesus taught, but
little on *how* he taught. Graduates replicate what they see
with classroom lectures, book studying, and passive learning
environments. But Jesus taught on the job. He lived, ate, and
traveled with the learners, continually interacting with them.
The Travel Team wasn't sightseeing; it was on a mission.
Learners got their hands dirty feeding crowds, licked their
wounds after a predictably difficult exorcism, and fell asleep
during late-night praying. They matriculated incarnationally,
which resulted in life change.

For eight years, my wife homeschooled our boys. During
a challenging afternoon, our youngest complained about his

life. Everything seemed miserable, including his schoolwork, brothers, parents, tennis, and friends. Without lecture or reprimand, my wife responded. She led him to the basement where we stored clothes bagged for the needy. My wife and son carried the sacks to the car and drove to a homeless shelter. They walked beside those with little, offering our clothes to the shelter. But the staff informed them that they weren't equipped to accept the donation, recommending a nearby thrift store instead.

"Okay, lesson learned," our son offered.

"Oh, we're not done," Nancy answered. "We still have to deliver our clothing." They drove to the store and unloaded the clothing.

"Okay, I get the point," our son said.

"Oh, we're not finished," his mom answered softly. Then they drove to a nursing home and asked if they could visit a resident who didn't have family or visitors. They spent an hour or two with an old woman, talking and listening.

"That's overkill," our son said. But he got the point, without yelling, lecture, or punishment. Experiences teach.

Active Learning

If you ask typical people about the most powerful life lessons they've learned, they'll nearly always tell you a story wrapped around an experience. When you engage the senses, not just cognition, the brain operates at a significantly different level, evoking emotions that become the glue for retention. The problem is that church leaders typically resort to a lecture method because it is easier, requires less effort, and is talent generated, relying on one or a few versus many. We exchange impact for control.

A few years ago, I received certification from the American Society of Training and Development, an association with nearly seventy thousand members. Many of these participants represent large corporations. The training focused on active learning, using visual devices, experiences, and techniques for getting people to interact with each other. Some studies show that retention goes up from 10 percent to nearly 90 percent when a person experiences information as opposed to merely hearing it. Another study focused on college lectures, contrasting a typical one with a class that took five minutes at the end for each student to interact with one another on what each learned. The latter group retained 70 percent more than the one where the students did not talk to each other.

Unfortunately, the typical church worship service is a come-and-listen event, where people sit, facing forward in long rows. I grew up learning that church was a place to be quiet, not to talk. I'd receive the evil eye or a flick of the earlobe from a parent, if caught talking to a friend. Church was a place to listen to others, just like school.

But Jesus rarely lectured. He invested a lot of time serving the needy, interacting with villagers, and modeling what he taught. Learners received on-the-job experience that resulted in skill development and heart change. Something happens within us when we go and do, not just sit and listen.

Adult Learning

Rick Rusaw, a pastor friend of mine, told me about a man who came to him one morning after church. "Can I get a prayer?" he asked.

"Sure," Rick said, assuming the man meant Rick praying for him.

When Rick moved into his prayer mode, the man said, "You don't understand. The prayer isn't for me. It's for a guy I met down at the halfway house," a home for recently released prisoners. Rick asked him what he meant.

The man said, "I went down to this house because my wife had volunteered. When I saw they needed some help fixing up the place, I started bringing my tools. Then a resident asked me why I was doing this, so I told him. He said, 'Could you pray for me?' I said, 'I don't know how to do that, but I know where I can get a prayer.' So I want you to write out a prayer so I can go back and pray for this guy."

Rick wrote a prayer and gave it to the man. He realized that this guy would never have attended a prayer workshop at the church, but because he was in a situation where someone called on him for prayer, he was now open to learning about praying for others. That's what an experiential environment provides: conditions fostering both skills and motivation.

While adults find it easier to understand how active learning works with children, they often fail to understand that it has little to do with age, but rather human nature. The big difference is that adults are far less likely to desire knowledge where there is no clear application to everyday life. They are not shopping for a solution for which they do not perceive a problem. Trying to teach unmotivated people is very difficult and retention is abysmal. But when you have engaged, curious participants, learning is a joy for both teacher and learner. The key is creating an environment where people yearn to learn. Experiences do that.

One day Jesus was praying. When he finished, one of his learners said, "Teach us to pray" (Luke 11:1). The request was a direct result of observing Jesus praying. The response was one of Jesus's most impacting lessons, commonly referred to as "The Lord's Prayer." Because the learners experienced Jesus praying, he'd piqued their curiosity and they wanted to know more.

Igniting Interest

I sat in a meeting where a friend told me about a new line of naturally sweet fruit drinks. His excitement about the new product caught my interest. "What does it taste like? Is it sweet or sour? Do they use natural juice or fructose? Does the drink taste best cool or iced? Is it dry or refreshing? Is it flat or fizzy? Is it . . . ?"

"Here," he said, sliding a drink toward me, "taste it yourself."

"Ahhh, that's really good!" I responded. "I'd like some more. What's the name of it? How much does it cost? I'll recommend this to my friends."

What happened in this conversation? The situation turned from informational to experiential. The experience answered my questions and provided a unique insight into the new drink that no amount of ingredient analysis or characteristic description could. Spiritual and character growth issues must become experiential if they are to be realized. Learning about God in a classroom or from a lecture method is equivalent to putting powdered milk on your cold cereal for breakfast. The basic nutrients are there but there's no heart, passion or taste. We can get what we need to survive from vitamins and pills but people still prefer food. Scripture tells us to "taste and see that the LORD is good" (Ps. 34:8).

When you analyze Jesus's method for soul growth, you see that he created significant experiences. Jesus responded to a doubting learner (Thomas) by saying, "Put your finger here; see my hands. Reach out your hand and put it into my side. Stop doubting and believe" (John 20:27). God took the prophet Isaiah through a multisensory event. Isaiah writes,

> In the year that King Uzziah died, I saw the LORD seated on a throne, high and exalted, and the train of his robe filled the temple. Above him were seraphs, each with six wings: With two wings they covered their faces, with two they covered their feet, and with two they were flying. And they were calling to one another: "Holy, holy, holy is the LORD Almighty; the whole earth is full of his glory." At the sound of their voices the doorposts and thresholds shook and the temple was filled with smoke. (Isa. 6:1–4)

Experience impacts the heart and passion. Show a child how to ride a bike in class and he'll be bored. Set him on the seat with his feet on the pedals and watch his eyes gleam. The first solo ride ignites the child, motivating him to ride more, faster, farther than before. People are far less interested in hearing about Jesus or a person's faith until after they've experienced an accepting, nonjudgmental conversation with the person. Don't mention God or Jesus until the other has witnessed your doing something unselfish, without an agenda. Don't serve to preach. Do it because you care. Serving is the new apologetics.

The Passion-Driven Life

Behaviors are not the end goal. That is legalism. Behavior as a means to growth promotes active learning, which spawns passion, whereas a passionless spiritual life is drudgery. Soul instruction loses energy when it is not accompanied by suitable application. Heart and passion engage the rest of our faculties at new levels of involvement. More than any single factor, passion changes lives, and changed lives transform the world.

In the Bible, Philip had a hard time convincing Nathanael about Jesus, so he simply said, "Come and see" (John 1:46).

Jesus taught servant leadership experientially. "He poured water into a basin and began to wash his disciples' feet, drying them with the towel that was wrapped around him" (John 13:5).

Faith takes on new meaning when applied experientially. "'Come,' [Jesus] said. Then Peter got down out of the boat, walked on the water and came toward Jesus" (Matt. 14:29).

Life is primarily experiential. Driving, golfing, marriage, sex, shopping, eating, and exercising are a tip of the active-learning iceberg. An experience creates a multisensory event that stimulates our minds as well as our emotions and bodies. It better reflects what God intended for us as complete beings, more than the intellectual assent of most soul growth methods that fail to ignite passion.

Travel Team Experiences

Jesus took his learners on a three-year road trip. While you may not be able to replicate this degree of experiential learning, your Travel Team will need to intentionally develop active learning opportunities. Part of the success and limitation of this type of learning is that you cannot always predict the outcomes of the participants' individual experiences. For the experiences to have their greatest effect, you need to make them as authentic as possible, requiring you to give up a certain amount of control.

Design

The design of a soul growth experience is important because a bad experience can prevent a person from learning an important truth. Haphazard, cheesy, or poorly designed learning opportunities can ruin the chances of subsequent soul growth. Grapevine conversations where people telegraph their sour experiences to others can discourage would-be participants. "Oh yeah, I went on one of those work projects and it was terrible. It was disorganized, a waste of my time." An effective soul growth experience creates an internal receptivity to a spiritual truth through external conditions. Scrimp on planning and harvest mediocrity.

What: A single event can result in multiple lessons based on the participants. You cannot guarantee what you and others will learn from an experience. However, if you are facilitating, consider what you *want* your Travel Team to experience. Do you want them to learn service, faith, missions, communication, or trust? Different goals require varying activities. If you do not have an objective in mind, outcomes may be haphazard, random, and disappointing. Experiences often teach multiple and varied truths, but it's important to begin with a focal point.

How: How do you plan to achieve these experiential goals? What circumstances will lead to such lessons? Why do you think this? Are you replicating what you've seen, or are you creating your own situation? Who are the participants? Are they young, old, male, female, new in the faith, or veterans? What time, budget, skills, talents, and tools do you have available? One challenge is finding the right need or situation that matches the available resources. Consider the opportunity to create an experiential moment within the course of a normal gathering, but also think about the life impact of a prolonged experience lasting anywhere from one day to ninety days, such as a weekend trip or short-term international mission.

Deploy

Preparation: Several of Jesus's recorded experiential activities required some preparation. Before feeding the thousands, a search was made for food and a little boy donated his sack lunch (John 6:8–9). Prior to the triumphal entry into Jerusalem, Jesus sent one of his learners to fetch a young colt that had been readied for such an event (Matt. 21:1–3). Before the Passover meal took place, Jesus apparently made arrangements to use someone's upper room and then asked his disciples to finish the task (Matt. 26:18–19). Spontaneous experiences can be effective, but soul growth methods often benefit from intentional preparation.

Implementation: Experiences can be fun, engaging, and memorable. We buy souvenirs and take pictures and videos as mementos of our experiences so we can relive them in part. During a planned experience, teachable moments— circumstances where learning is optimal—often arise. Such fertile conditions increase growth, so long as they are recognized and seized. Even when an event fails, a teachable moment often emerges that results in significant learning. The successful execution of the event should not take precedence over teachable moments.

For example, a Travel Team I was a part of had planned a weekend retreat. The event had been on our calendars for months. A week before, a family member of one of the men died. The same week, another member lost his job and felt he should stay to support his family. We postponed the retreat. But the interruptions not only gave us opportunity to care for our members, they created an environment for deep discussion on disappointments and the fragility of life.

Debrief

That leads us to one of the biggest wastes in experiences: failing to intentionally unpack thoughts, feelings, and learnings after the event itself. Skipping the debrief is tempting when you are pressed for time, tired from the experience itself, or merely overlooking the importance. Three direct benefits come from taking the time and effort after an event to stir conversation and gather feedback. (1) You get to hear what other Travel Team members experienced, gaining different perspectives and deepening the community among them. (2) Other participants sharpen insights they gleaned that may be vague without debriefing. Facilitators can use the experience to illustrate a key point. Follow-up discussion improves clarity and impact as talking articulates your ideas. (3) You gather immediate input that can improve future experience design. Usually, immediate feedback is the most accurate. Time has a way of fading and skewing the experience.

One of the most important aspects of experiential learning is participant discussion. You can see how little this takes place in the typical mass or church service, where we're lectured to as passive participants. The power of discussion is not so much what we learn from others. Talking forces us to think at a deeper level as we feel the responsibility of articulating our thoughts in a social setting. This heightens learning and increases retention.

Why did we do this? Revisit the purpose of the experience. Did it accomplish its objectives? Why or why not? In addition to hearing potential lessons and life applications gained by the participants, this feedback provides information for the experience planner to see what can be done to improve it for others.

What/How: What did each participant gain from the experience? What lasting impact might this have on how we live our lives, work together, or view God? "It was fun" is hardly a worthwhile assessment by itself. If the goal was to experience community, that's one thing. If it was to learn a healthy way of letting go of stress, that is another. Again, an experience for entertainment's sake is not the objective of soul growth. Entertainment literally means "to hold in tension." Most effective communication in an entertainment-laden society must contain elements of attention holding. But entertainment should be a means and by-product, not the primary goal. A residual benefit is the goal of a soul growth experience, not just the event itself. That goal, ultimately, is to increase SI. To hold a person's attention for no other purpose than to entertain, while popular and lucrative, has little benefit to the human race.

Crafting effective debriefing questions is not easy. Jesus frequently taught Socratically, using questions as catalysts for new thinking. Avoid questions that can be answered with one-word responses. Try to capture deeper learnings that often require discussion about emotions, feelings, and relationships, typically more challenging for men, until they become more familiar with the process. Keep pushing back with "Why?" or "Tell me more" or "What does that look like in your life?" These coaching questions do not likely have pat answers. Push back on canned responses. You're not looking for Sunday school answers or factual content. You want to develop spiritual thinking, not religious regurgitation.

Simulated Experiences

A growing number of training situations include simulated scenarios, where the high cost of time, resources, and risk make live training prohibitive. An example of this is flight simulators, where pilots experience a cockpit with controls, motions, and computer-generated weather and instrument conditions in order to develop and test their responses. Creating short, synthetic, convenient experiences in Travel Team gatherings can raise the level of soul growth.

A synthetic exercise is one that has indirect, real-world applications, but is something we'd find inside a controlled learning environment. Examples of these are a ropes obstacle course, a backpack trip, or any number of training games that can be accomplished in five to thirty minutes of a regularly scheduled meeting. The latter can be found in a variety of training game books as well as high-priced executive development course manuals. You can implement these conveniently and with limited time, cost, and organization. Backdoor learning involves teaching via a game or activity that does not appear educational in nature. Benefits of synthetic experiences are greater control, less time investment, and thus a larger number of opportunities to learn on a variety of themes. You might think of these as experiential parables. Jesus often taught in parables, stories that were symbolic with real-world implications. An active learning experience is similar in that it is representative of a skill or life lesson that is taught in an encapsulated format.

My work in KidLead (www.kidlead.com) implements a large number of these, accomplished during club meetings. Young leaders work on competitive challenges that are fun and interactive, but that teach enduring skills that can easily be adapted in real-world situations outside of the more controlled environment. The result is significant skill development for effective, ethical leading, allowing future influencers to get a ten- to twenty-year head start.

Four Experiential Examples

Inner-city mission trip

Design: The Bible tells us to show compassion to the poor and disadvantaged. A Travel Team I was involved with in Arizona wanted to create an opportunity where people in the more affluent Scottsdale could practice this. We contacted the Phoenix Rescue Mission, with whom our church had an ongoing relationship, and scheduled a date for our covenant group members and their families to serve food to homeless people and help conduct a worship service after dinner.

Deploy: The last Sunday of the month, we carpooled to the Phoenix inner city and made ourselves available to the Phoenix Rescue Mission staff for food preparation, service, and the after-dinner worship meeting.

Debrief: After the event, we gathered for ten minutes before leaving the mission compound and discussed questions such as these: "What did you learn from this experience?" "How did you feel while serving dinner?" "Did you have an opportunity to connect with a specific individual who stood out to you?" "How will this affect your everyday life?" "Would you like to schedule another trip to the Rescue Mission?"

Teaching a devotional

Design: Leading a brief Bible study should not be relegated solely to pastors/priests. Many opportunities allow you to share an instructional and encouraging word from Scripture. The goal is to give everyone an opportunity to experience leading a devotional that is based on the Bible, in front of a friendly group of four to six friends.

Deploy: Have the Path Finder model two to three lessons. Teach an instructional lesson on creating and presenting a devotional for the members of a Travel Team. Each person is scheduled to teach during a gathering.

Debrief: Affirm the teacher and share as a group after the person's devotional. As the group leader, I follow this up with personal feedback and ask the teacher questions such as, "What was the most challenging part of the process?" "Did you enjoy it?" "Why or why not?" "Do you think that it prepared you to do this sort of service again?"

Single mother home fix-up

Design: Scripture emphasizes the importance of taking care of widows and orphans. My group learned about a woman in our church who was a single, full-time working mother with two teenage boys. Her divorce was pending, and the father was an alcoholic who did not help her with the boys or with fixing up the house. We wanted to live out these scriptural principles by helping this woman fix her house.

Deploy: We asked the woman to put together a list of items that needed repair, so that we could gather the proper tools, resources, and expertise before our work. Then we set a date to meet as a group at her house.

Debrief: At our next group meeting after the workday, we discussed questions such as, "How did you feel about helping this woman?" "What was meaningful and what was frustrating?" "Why do you think Scripture talks so much about taking care of the widows and orphans?" "How can we do this better as a faith community?"

Cemetery walk

Design: The book of Ecclesiastes says that life is full of meaningless activities and passes quickly. One way to teach this experientially is to take a field trip to a local cemetery and walk among the graves. Allow time at the beginning for people to walk around (ten to fifteen minutes) and perhaps even challenge them to look for the oldest grave, the oldest person, someone with a birth date near theirs, or a creative saying on a gravestone. The goal is to create a sense of urgency regarding what is really important in life.

Deploy: My group has done this activity as a surprise event, thus eliminating the possibility that some members might feel anxious beforehand about the idea of walking through a cemetery. We've also done it with everyone knowing, creating a sense of curiosity and anticipation of this activity. We carpool to the cemetery and give everyone instructions, including a meeting time and place.

Debrief: We processed our experience together with questions such as, "What did you see and feel as you walked around?" "What is on your bucket list (things you'd like to do before you 'kick the bucket')?" "What would you like to give up doing that seems to be taking a lot of time or energy but doesn't seem worth your while?"

Examples of Simulated Experiential Learning Ideas

- In an outdoor setting, give members an opportunity to do a short walk to find an item that symbolizes where they are in their spiritual walk, and then do a show-and-tell. People select things such as rocks, old leaves, twigs, new leaves, dirt clumps, etc.
- Wrap up a lesson on trusting God as the source of forgiveness, peace, and faith by setting up three pitchers of water with a sign on each. One says "forgiveness," another "peace," and the third "faith." At the end, Travel Team members are invited to take a water cup, fill and drink it from the container that matches their current need.

- Watch a movie clip (one to five minutes) that depicts a scene representing a theme you've been discussing and use it as a conversation catalyst. For example, a talk on leadership or bravery might be emphasized with the scene from *Braveheart* where William Wallace challenges the army to take a risk.

- Play a round of Pictionary, where a person draws a picture without talking or gestures to get the others to guess the word or phrase. Select words and phrases that tie into the theme of the meeting's Directions, or use it to share the challenges of communicating in marriage.

- Select a fifty- to one-hundred-piece jigsaw puzzle, but remove two or three pieces and/or replace them with pieces from another puzzle. Put the puzzle together as you share the events of the week from your lives. Then at the end, talk about what's missing in your life right now, or share a time in your past when the pieces didn't seem to come together. Where was God in the process? How did you respond? What did you learn from it?

- During a theme on sharing faith and developing a burden for people who seem lost in their connection with God, invite each person to light a candle for a specific person or persons, symbolizing their commitment to share their spiritual light as well as to pray for the person's soul growth.

- On a Travel Team member's birthday, take that person out for breakfast and have each person sign a card, writing one or two specific things that they admire and respect about that individual.

- Take a photo of the Travel Team, frame a copy for each person, and present them as a prayer reminder of the group, perhaps during the last meeting time of the covenant. People tend to display these in prominent places. Covenant to reunite periodically or to gather for an annual reunion.

Summary

Jesus used experiential, interactive communication to create a learning environment that was engaging and effective. Travel Teams benefit from doing the same. Sitting and listening in large group events or lounging in a small group setting limits growth when it is the sole or dominant method. Accomplishing work projects, experiencing a road trip or retreat, and participating in multisensory activities combined with robust discussion and debriefing are far more effective means for stimulating learning. Seeing how people respond in a variety of competitive, stressful settings provides windows into their lives, assisting in their growth. SI results as we combine experiential learning with our soul growth methods.

Interaction Ideas:

1. What is one thing you got out of this chapter?

2. Why do you think it is more productive to do experiences in the context of the same group (Travel Team) each time, rather than separately or with other groups of people?

3. Emotions are like glue for remembering a truth or experience. Share an important life lesson you learned in your past and describe the emotions surrounding that event.

4. Brainstorm a few activities you could do that might provide learning for a biblical truth.

Activity: Provide fifty index cards and tape, and challenge your team members to build the tallest freestanding tower they can in five minutes. Then provide another fifty cards, taking away the tape and challenging the team to build the tallest tower they can in five minutes. What happens when changes take place in our lives? What is a change that required you to do life differently than you'd done before? What did you learn from it? How was doing this activity more impacting than merely talking about the concept of changes, or even describing the activity and then discussing it intellectually?

SEVEN

The Path Finder

Increasing Your Rate of Growth and Avoiding Plateaus

The fourth element of Jesus's method for acquiring spiritual intelligence is a Path Finder. A Path Finder is a person who provides support and insights that assist you or a Travel Team in making progress on your journey. A Path Finder also benefits from his or her role, which catalyzes further growth and maturation. Such a person often serves as a great navigator, initiating group life and facilitating Directions discussions.

Remember, four elements create synergy to facilitate SI. The Travel Team provides the vehicle for your journey. Experiencing the Trip becomes the fuel. The Directions are the road map or GPS. But sometimes, maps are difficult to read. The scale is left out or does not take into account road construction, rush-hour traffic, or detours. Anyone who has used MapQuest or a GPS system more than a few times knows this challenge. In these cases, getting directions from a local makes a big difference, someone who knows the territory and can give you the scoop on a shortcut or on steering clear of a bad route.

As learners, we grow significantly by others' pouring into our lives. As Path Finders, our growth comes as we pour into the lives of others. It's a mutual benefit, because a Path

Finder becomes one of the participants. As we've noted, the biggest single reason for the lack of spiritual maturity among followers is utilizing the wrong methods. The second is that so few take on the responsibility of Path Finding. Instead, we depend on a few trained professionals, teaching to the masses. People only grow to a certain level with such methods.

The Art of Path Finding

Jesus served as the Path Finder in his Travel Team. He suggested in his farewell to his learners that they replicate this method (Matt. 28:16–20). A Path Finder is part mentor, teacher, parent, coach, and friend. None of these in and of itself accurately describes a Path Finder, but together they paint a picture of one. Because most of us have little experience with this role, we find it easier to understand the concept in comparison with more familiar ones.

Path Finding is an invaluable means for spiritual formation, learning, and personal growth. The art of Path Finding has become less and less a part of our culture due to mobility, generational distinctions, loss of community, and dysfunctional family settings. A perceived replacement for Path Finding is education, whereby a system of classrooms, curriculum, and low- or non-relational learning conditions inclines us to think we can obtain wisdom through information alone. Another common substitute for Path Finding is professional counseling, paying someone to help us manage our journey. While Path Finding is therapeutic, and therapy can unlock spiritual discovery, these are different processes.

A Path Finder tends to have more experience, maturity, and willingness to speak into another's life. A Path Finder is not a teacher, merely transferring information to another. A Path Finder is not a consultant: "Here's what I did in this situation and here's what I think you should do." There is some of that, but it involves more of an insightful presence than specific recommendations. A Path Finder is not a life coach, because a good coach may have little experience or maturity but has skills for asking strategic questions that unlock a "coachee's" potential. While a good Path Finder often uses coaching techniques, a certain amount of experience is required from which to draw wisdom and insights.

A Path Finder is most like a mentor among these more familiar descriptions. The big difference is that mentors usually function in a one-on-one relationship. A Path Finder works with a Travel Team, involving more than one person. Since a Travel Team is an intentional, covenantal relationship, a Path Finder often initiates interaction with a group of people invited to form a Travel Team. There are a growing number of books and resources on mentoring and becoming a spiritual director that can be adapted for those willing to serve as Path Finders. Group dynamics change how people interact with the mentor or spiritual guide.

A Path Finder facilitates conversation that includes a spiritual dimension to life issues. As issues arise among Travel Team members, the Path Finder can help the group go deeper, exploring possible solutions that clarify a person's thinking. At times, a Path Finder may share intuitions if a person seems stuck or on the verge of making a bad decision. After trust has been earned, a Path Finder may need to confront a person going down the wrong path, similar to a person grabbing a friend about to step in front of a car. For the most part, a Path Finder is available to "be" with others, gently speaking out of his or her experiences as teachable moments arise. This is the agenda: to be present as the Travel Team experiences life together.

Path Finding is about coming alongside people for the primary purpose of helping them discover God in their journey. As a spiritual director, you catalyze thinking about God, spirituality, and discovering one's purpose in eternity. Although primary, this is not your sole purpose. As soon as you make it such, you decrease your impact. That's why typical religious training and worship services do not bring about spiritual intelligence. When they become our singular source for soul growth, they lose the context of everyday life, becoming compartmentalized experiences and content.

Jesus did not provide a constant string of programs and events. Rather, he walked through a variety of experiences with his learners. They more than likely shot the breeze around a campfire, told jokes, laughed when someone passed gas, discussed local politics, predicted the next day's weather, and negotiated who'd wash the clothes and prepare lunch. When arguments arose over position, accomplishing tasks, or setting priorities, Jesus provided salient questions or Directions to ponder. These were teachable moments. Periodically he'd introduce key concepts and parables, creating discussions as they walked to the next village. There were no fill-in-the-blank notes to tuck away in their scrolls until the next week's lecture. Path Finding is both organic and intentional. The agenda is growth, not accomplishing a specific curriculum.

A Path Finder is one who is farther along the path, but who walks beside us in our journey. She or he kindly, gently, and vulnerably shares ideas, failures, discoveries, and wisdom as the rest of us strive to take the next step. Our conversations might center on work, home, marriage, parenting, health, and any number of other themes, not just God.

As we serve as a Path Finder, we develop others to become Path Finders. Eleven of the twelve learners Jesus journeyed with became powerful leaders within a mere three years after joining Jesus's Travel Team. They didn't have special sessions on Path Finding or classes on the ten things needed to help someone along his or her journey. Rather, they watched, experienced, discussed, and then replicated.

Benefits

Path Finding may appear to be an optional element in spiritual intelligence methods, but don't underestimate its impact. The

Path Finder is a catalyst, increasing one's speed toward maturity. How fast a person progresses is often a direct result of making right choices, avoiding wrong decisions, and applying Directions effectively—the primary benefits of a Path Finder's guidance. Here are some reasons why this happens.

View from around the bend: While hindsight is not 20/20 because it is skewed by misperceptions, time lag, and change in context, it is more helpful than no experience at all. History repeats itself because people must learn certain life lessons on their own. But we can avert some learning by gleaning from others' experiences. A Path Finder sees from a vantage point that is a bit farther down the road, providing perspective that helps others.

While pastoring, I did premarital counseling. The adage is true: "You can tell a young man in love, but you can't tell him much." The real strength of premarital counseling, like good Path Finding, is that it prepares learners for what is ahead, as much or more than addressing current issues. Knowing the signs of a heart attack can help a potential victim get immediate help and not pass the pain off as a reaction to late-night eating. Because wisdom cannot be gained by merely reading a book and hearing a lecture, an experienced Path Finder provides invaluable, preparatory guidance.

A model to watch: One antismoking commercial showed a dad and son sitting in a park, leaning against a tree. The father took a cigarette out of a pack and lit up. The son, looking at his father, reached for the pack on the ground and began to take out a cigarette. The unspoken message is that people do as people see done. As social beings, we tend to replicate what we observe. Styles, fads, brands, verbiage, and popularity movements are born and change. By establishing a relationship with learners, the power of modeling is a natural result of Path Finding.

One morning during one of our group meetings with Ray Ortlund, a few of us were caught up in critiquing the latest televangelist scandal. Ray was the president of the National

Religious Broadcasters at the time, so it seemed a bit odd for him to remain so silent on the matter. At a pause in our debate, Ray said softly, "We're all just one step away from scandal, aren't we?" The deathly silence was probably no different than the times Jesus kindly confronted his learners. I don't think I've criticized a pastoral failure since then. Ray's modeling in the matter taught what content and lecture could not.

Real-world application: A gap typically exists between what we know and what we do. It is no more evident than in the arena of character and spiritual growth. Teaching provides information, but "how to" is missing in most classroom education.

If you're a dad like me, you cringe when you see those unfortunate words on the box of a gift your child unwraps: "Some Assembly Required." Watching someone else put a contraption together beats any instruction booklet. Spiritual intelligence is about applying what we learn. Path Finders provide a valuable connection between ideas and applications, thoughts and actions, *should do* and *how to*. Through the course of a year or two, your Travel Team will experience significant events, lived firsthand or vicariously through the others in the group. This life lab tests theory, allowing us to experience challenges in close community. The Path Finder facilitates deeper understanding at strategic moments.

Credible accountability: Another benefit of Path Finding is experiencing Mutually Earned Accountability with a person who has gained credibility because of his or her life wisdom. Mutual accountability among peers does not have the same degree of accountability, because any one person may not be as experienced or in a position to provide improvement ideas. Path Finding suggests things that work, a best practices approach to life and spirituality, warning us about deadends and flawed methods that only come from the seasoning of life.

Selecting a Path Finder

How do you find a suitable Path Finder? Chances are you'll have to do the asking, since most people are not in tune with this process or feel inadequate for the role. Consider what you are looking for in such a relationship. Haphazard Path Finding can be frustrating as well as ineffective. Choose well. Here are some ideas to ponder as you think of potential people to ask.

Need/Strength Match: What do you need to learn or develop? Where are you lacking? Look for someone who has more experience in an area where you want to grow, such as leading, managing, theology, exercise, investing, or more general life wisdom. What can this person potentially offer you in terms of information and insight, based on his or her experience? Try to think through what it is you want to accomplish before establishing such a relationship.

Model: You don't want to merely find someone who knows more than you. Seek a person who exhibits qualities you admire. Beware placing a person on too high of a pedestal. Such a relationship will inevitably disappoint you. Paul wrote, "We did this, not because we do not have the right to such help, but in order to make ourselves a model for you to follow" (2 Thess. 3:9).

> Teach the older women to be reverent in the way they live, not to be slanderers or addicted to much wine, but to teach what is good. Then they can train the younger women to love their husbands and children, to be self-controlled and pure, to be busy at home, to be kind, and to be subject to their husbands, so that no one will malign the word of God. . . . In everything set them an example by doing what is good. (Titus 2:3–5, 7)

Availability: No matter how wonderful of a Path Finder you find, if you cannot mesh schedules, it's not going to work. The busyness of life and geographical challenges can be significant barriers. While email, video conferencing, and cell phones can help, nothing beats face-to-face interaction. Responsibility for finding suitable time should be the burden of the ones being developed. While my wife was on staff with leadership guru John Maxwell, I asked him if we could spend time together so I could learn from his ministry and leadership experiences. Because of his busy schedule, we only had an opportunity to meet in his office once or twice. On other occasions, I drove the car for him on the way to a speaking event or the airport. These times provided opportunities to talk, listen, and just "be" together.

The Ask: The next big task is the "ask." The fear of rejection is strong in most of us. But you will be surprised how many people—even powerful, busy ones—are willing to become Path Finders if asked. Establishing an initial contact personally or through a friend is probably necessary. Communicate what you are looking for in terms of time and topic, assuring the potential Path Finder—especially if the person is busy—that his or her investment will be appreciated and well used.

Learner as Path Finder

Jesus served as his learners' Path Finder. The obvious benefit was that they gained significantly from his knowledge, modeling, and inside track to understanding God. But here's a twist, a potentially controversial one for some. What if Jesus became a Path Finder partly for his own spiritual development, to aid the practices of prayer, fasting, and Scripture in his personal growth? As I mentioned, one of my early Path Finders was Ray Ortlund, a veteran pastor, author, and radio personality. One time we asked him why he invested his time with us—there was no money involved, and it wasn't a part of his job description. His response startled me: "I do this for me. I need this," Ray said. At the time I chalked up the response to Ray's humble attitude. But I've come to realize he was right. We were as much a part of Ray's continued spiritual growth as he was ours, even though he was far more mature and experienced than the rest of us. That is the mutual benefit of the Path Finder's role.

In graduate school, I studied communication psychology, an interdisciplinary program involving coursework in both fields. My advisor was a professor who'd written a pithy and practical textbook called *Messages That Work*, dealing with designing effective messages. During my second year, my professor became ill and could not finish teaching an undergraduate course that was based on his textbook. Because I'd done well in his course, I was asked to finish teaching his class. I quickly discovered I was in over my head. I learned as much or more teaching the subject as I did as a student, because I had to prepare lectures and field students' questions.

There comes a time in nearly everyone's journey when, unless you begin Path Finding with others, you'll hit a plateau, in spite of continued acquisition of Directions and serving in other areas. This is the cycle of spiritual intelligence. As I write this book, I am forty-nine. By the time it is published, I'll have turned fifty. Psychologists tell us that around the age of fifty, generativity starts. This is the phase of life where people begin focusing on leaving a legacy, often by investing in future generations.

In a similar theme, business teachers refer to an S-curve, a universal product and organizational cycle.

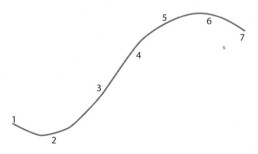

Each point signifies a different stage in the life of an organism or organization. If at Point 5, another idea or innovation is not begun, the product or organization will begin to plateau and decline, getting to a point where renewal is impossible and death is imminent. As a church growth consultant, I realize there are literally tens of thousands of congregations and dozens of denominations at Point 7 on the curve. No matter how much investment goes into them, they will never experience new life. The responsibility is to prepare to die, hopefully leaving a legacy of resources to those capable of new growth.

The cycle of spiritual intelligence is not so much chronological as it is developmental. There will come a time in your soul's growth that for you to continue, you'll need to start assisting others in their journey. The idea is not that you get done learning and then become a teacher. That's the educational model—conquer the content and then disperse it to others. Tenured professors who regurgitate lesson content year after year don't help themselves or their students. Spiritual intelligence is about employing the methods that help us obtain maturity. The process of joining others in their journey makes ours dynamic and different.

On the occasion that Path Finding loses its challenge, you might consider one of three alternatives. There may be a relational mismatch, where you just don't have good chemistry with your team. Don't fret, just graciously transition to a new group as appropriate. You may also change up your style a bit, in case your approach has become too routine for you. A third option is pursuing more challenging Travel Team members, whether that means more or less spiritually mature, or different in terms of age and culture.

Getting Started

"Oh, but you don't know me," some might say. "I'm not a teacher. I'm not a leader." You may not be ready. Although growth is more a matter of quality than quantity, my estimate is that a person who's been active in a healthy church for at least three years is ready to begin Path Finding. Consider less time if you've been in a healthy Travel Team, because your growth will have been more rapid.

But more often, I hear this hesitancy when a person has a mistaken idea of what a Path Finder does. Path Finding is not about teaching a Bible study, counseling, or leading in an organizational sense. It is about being yourself among a small group of people, sharing stories of your life and lessons you've learned. This isn't a place for preaching little sermons, critiquing others, or figuring out who you can recruit into your new business scheme. Rather, your "job" is to caringly and humbly interact with a few who want to grow spiritually. Don't underestimate your life experiences and how your struggles can become an aid to others.

Serving as a mentor one-on-one is beneficial, but being a Path Finder on a Travel Team has greater value. One-on-one discipleship has the weakness of the learner's temptation to become dependent on the mentor and overly influenced by that person. The tempering of a Travel Team, consisting of a variety of personalities, experiences, and relationship dynamics, provides a healthier context for a Path Finder, not to mention multiplying your time and energy investment. As far as we know, Jesus did not invest a lot of time one-on-one.

Chances are that people will not come up to you and ask you to consider being their Path Finder. Because so few employ these methods of spiritual intelligence, you'll likely need to initiate a Travel Team. The best place to begin is to look for people who are younger than you, either chronologically, emotionally, spiritually, or a combination of these. In some situations, you could have a twenty-five-year-old serving as Path Finder with a group of midlifers, if that person's development warranted it. But usually, a group will be an older Path Finder with younger learners in terms of years, because what we're looking for is not just an awareness of Directions, but also life experience. These are difficult to learn from a book or to fake. The issue is not, "Do I have Path Finding in me?" You will if you want to keep progressing in your spiritual journey. The issue becomes more a matter of how you structure it and the type of people in your Travel Team. Some Path Finders may want to focus on preteens or youth. Others may invite collegians and young adults. Still others may want to work with midlifers and older adults. You may feel more comfortable with less educated and manual workers. Others may prefer higher capacity leaders. Consider finding your niche in the who and how, more than deliberating whether or not you should be a Path Finder.

Many who are ready to begin Path Finding may feel unready. The natural progression is to begin with a small Travel Team that you facilitate as a Path Finder, while you're still in a different Travel Team as a participant. As you progress in your journey, you'll move more and more of your time and energy into Path Finding. You may want to hone your skills with peer Path Finders or select a Path Finder who can mentor you.

I was in such a relationship with a man who had been the president of the university I attended. (His son wrote the foreword of this book.) We met every month or so for breakfast to shoot the breeze, discuss life, and whatever else we wanted to talk about. I was forty-five while he was approaching eighty. While I was honored to enjoy the friendship and wisdom from a man this notable, I could tell that he enjoyed his time with me as well. His life had slowed considerably from his active years. Not long after that, he passed away. My life is different because of our time together. While the number of your potential Path Finders decreases with age and maturity, you will be able to find people who can speak into your life and help you progress.

The best teachers are often just one step ahead of you, and the best learners are one step behind. The person one step ahead still remembers what it's like to be where you are and is most apt to show you how he got to the next step. The reason that the person one step behind is the best student is because she or he can identify with the person ahead and better understand the next step to take. The greater the distance between teacher and learner, the more difficult it is at times to communicate effectively. You probably won't be able to find a Billy Graham or Mother Teresa to become your Path Finder, but chances are you can identify someone who is a step or two ahead of you for the next leg in your journey. If it is your time to begin Path Finding, look around and you'll find those who will benefit from your involvement in their life.

Next Steps

Preparation: The best preparation to become a Path Finder yourself is to have experienced a positive relationship with one. Replicating what you observe is the best approach. If you've not benefited from having a good Path Finder, you may want to practice in another area of leadership first. A significant amount of spiritual growth takes place when we switch places from receiver to giver. In our local church, we had numerous people young in their faith who became teachers in the children's ministry. They discovered this to be a wonderful means of spiritual growth, because they had to prepare Bible lessons they would not otherwise learn.

Inviting Learners: Perhaps the most difficult task in becoming a Path Finder is aligning with learners who are eager, willing, and available to make the commitment. Rarely should a Path Finder "sell" himself to a potential learner. You can raise the idea of such a relationship, but don't bait the hook. Desire to learn is nine-tenths of any Travel Team relationship. You may want to begin by asking potential Travel Team members to read this book with you.

Path Finder Maturity: Perhaps the greatest single quality of being a good Path Finder has less to do with spirituality and Bible knowledge than it does emotional intelligence. Because a Path Finder relationship places one person in a role of influence with another, a person's emotional disposition can do or undo positive spiritual influence. A person who is not healthy should not allow themselves to be in a position of guiding another. A person who lacks self-identity, emotional stability, and basic common sense will prove to be an unreliable Path Finder.

Disappointment: Path Finding is not for the easily discouraged person. More times than not, you will be disappointed by people in whom you've poured much time and effort. Leading a Travel Team is a labor of love that will help you grow, sometimes through disappointments. Some learners will become a Judas to you. Some Travel Teams never gel. Members may not bond.

When Jesus's disciples could not exorcise a demon, stay awake at a crucial time for prayer, respond to each other in humility, exude faith, or stay calm during a storm, Jesus felt frustrated. But he turned these situations into learning opportunities. When a learner disappoints you, talk about it. Learners have free will and will make decisions on their own, regardless of your advice or wisdom. Paul admitted, "I fear for you, that somehow I have wasted my efforts on you. I plead with you, brothers, become like me, for I became like you. You have done me no wrong" (Gal. 4:11–12). Jesus knew what it was like to heal ten lepers and only have one say "thanks." Don't expect a lot of fanfare or accolades. Path Finding tends to be a low-key, behind-the-scenes activity with inherent risks, but the potential payoffs are well worth it. Handling the disappointments of Travel Team members betraying you or flaking out has as much to do with your growth as your Path Finding has to do with their growth.

Start now to consider who might become a Path Finder in your life. To ask someone to do this is one of the greatest honors you can pay another person. Consider the idea of serving as a Path Finder for a Travel Team. Your goal is not to teach, but rather to be an encourager as you nudge others forward and share your journey with them.

Summary

You now have the four elements that make up the SI methods Jesus used to grow souls. By combining a Travel Team with Directions, Experiencing the Trip, and including a Path Finder, you have an environment most conducive to soul growth and maturation. Again, you don't have to use the terms we're using in this book. Call them what you want or nothing at all, but be sure to stay true to the essence of all four SI methods. I've intentionally avoided using familiar terms because they so often reflect attitudes and actions that fall short of the way Jesus used them. In the second section of this book, you'll learn various ways to apply these methods and to improve them as you go.

Interaction Ideas:

1. What is one thing you got out of this chapter?

2. Why do you think people are so fearful of becoming a Path Finder in others' lives?

3. On a 1–5 scale, 1 being not ready at all to be a Path Finder and 5 being overly ready, what number would you give yourself and why?

4. Name one or two people who could serve you as a Path Finder or to whom you could be a Path Finder.

Activity: Chances are you won't have these available, but if you do, get four used or inexpensive chairs. Cut three legs off of one, two legs off another, and one leg off a third. Then take turns sitting on each of the four chairs.

If you don't have access to chairs you can destroy, have everyone stand on one leg. Then walk around and gently push people until they use two legs. Then have them stand on two legs, and gently push them again. Then have people partner up, with one of them standing on one foot only. Then have the partners hold onto each other with all fours firmly on the ground.

What was the difference between one, two, three, and four legs? How is this similar to the process of using all four SI methods?

Section II

Planning Your Trip

EIGHT

Reading the Odometer

Measuring Your Progress While Avoiding Legalism

Thanks to Photoshop software, your picture can be digitally placed in front of a lot of different backdrops, giving the appearance that you're traveling without ever having to leave home. But an authentic journey will manifest itself in tangible ways. Many well-meaning people spin their tires in spiritual activities, never traveling far. In spite of sermon notes, Bible study booklets, and three-ring conference binders, they find themselves only a short distance down the trail. As a coastal Californian, I know all too well that you should not equate time in the car with proximity to the destination. So how do you know if you're making progress on your journey? What does SI look like?

Faux Fruit

On a family vacation to the Bahamas, we visited the Straw Market in Nassau, where the cruise ships drop their passengers for brief visits. A large tent houses scores of Bahamian merchants, mostly women, each with a few square feet of space, crowding narrow aisles. There they pitch souvenirs and brand-name imitations at negotiable prices to would-be buyers. A common ware is purses by alleged designers such as Coach, Yves Saint Laurent, Dolce & Gabbana, and Prada. You can dicker the price down to $60, $50, and $35, a fraction of a genuine item. Although they look like the high-priced originals, they're imitations, knockoffs. Now, when our family sees a woman with a Coach purse, we don't assume it's real. We whisper to each other, "Looks like she's been to the Bahamas."

That's a similar response to when people see others bearing faux spiritual fruit. The word *faux* is a French word for "fake," giving it a classier sound. But imitation is imitation. Judgmental, self-righteous, preachy, legalistic, and pious attitudes are symptomatic of low SI. Jesus accused religious leaders of his day of others-demeaning attitudes that were substitutes for the real thing. No wonder there is growing disgust toward church-goers and Christian zealots who exude knockoff qualities of faith. You don't have to be an expert to detect a fake.

Genuine SI is endearing. People are attracted to authentic soul growth. The crowds thronged after Jesus. There is a natural like-ability of those with SI. Genuine maturity is attractive. Unable to articulate why, people are naturally drawn toward high-SI individuals, regardless of personality, looks, or socioeconomic status. These qualities transcend philosophical, ethnic, or gender differences that tend to divide us when SI is missing.

SI Behavitudes

SI is evident in the presence of certain "behavitudes." I introduce the concept of a behavitude in my book *The Power of a New Attitude*, which discusses how we limit ourselves and how we can improve by making a few key adjustments. A behavitude is a combination of behavior and attitude; the two are significantly linked.

I grew up in a strict, religious culture that considered card playing, theatergoing, coed swimming, dancing, drinking alcohol, and smoking sins. Some went so far as to suggest that attending carnivals, bowling, or even reading the Sunday paper was ungodly. We didn't even think of going shopping on the Sabbath. These legalistic standards initially made sense for the well-intended leaders who established them, but they eventually became burdensome external rules. The problem with rule teaching is that we have to keep changing the list as culture evolves. For example, some labeled it wrong to go to movies, but when videos and cable television became available, people watched questionable material in the privacy of their homes. Instead of teaching the value of filling our minds with wholesome material, we focused on an external rule. Someone said a hypocrite is a person who complains about the sex and violence on his DVD player. Two people can avoid a behavior, but one for healthy, spiritual reasons and the other with unhealthy, legalistic motives.

SI goes beyond behaviors into the nitty-gritty issues of motives, intent, and attitudes. According to Jesus, the ultimate outcome of spiritual maturity is to love God with all your heart and to love your neighbor as yourself (Matt. 22:36–39). The genuine expression is love, joy, peace, patience, kindness, goodness, faithfulness, gentleness, and self-control (Gal. 5:22–23). Most people can fake manifestations of these attitudes temporarily, but not on a consistent basis.

If I handed you a sponge filled with milk and told you to squeeze it, milk would come out of it. If I asked, "Why did milk come out of the sponge?" you might say, "Because I squeezed it."

Perhaps, but milk came out primarily because milk was in the sponge. If water were in the sponge, water would come out. If oil were in the sponge, oil would come out. When people, work, traffic, and bills squeeze us, what comes out is what's in us. Stress reveals character, who we are on the inside.

360°

One of the best ways to improve your SI is getting feedback from others, as we suggest in The Journey. The reason is that growth is most evident in measuring the difference between "before" and "after," instead of taking a single snapshot at any point along the way. To determine growth, people need to know us awhile, observing us in a variety of situations, as in a Travel Team. If you only rely on what those who see you in church or a Bible study say about you, the feedback you receive will be only marginally helpful.

From time to time, I consult with churches. Many have the perception that they are friendly. You will hear their leaders say, "One of our strengths is our friendliness." But when we visit without anyone knowing us, we find quite the opposite. While members act friendly toward each other, outsiders feel the opposite. Yet congregants truly believe they're a friendly church.

Self-perception leads to deception. Studies show that over 90 percent of people believe they are above average in getting along with others, and a majority think they are better looking than most. When assessing SI, get feedback from a variety of people, including your supervisor at work, those who report to you, peers, neighbors, relatives, and people inside and outside your faith community. This will give you a broad, 360-degree perspective to evaluate your growth. SI and behavitudes are trans-situational. They carry over from setting to setting.

Switchbacks

Our journeys are more like a mountain trail with switchbacks than a stairway or a straight road. As you progress along the path, you'll begin to notice similar scenery. If the scenery never changes, chances are you're not progressing, merely marching in place. You may simply be going from relationship to relationship, job to job, or hurt to hurt. These are signs of not growing.

There's another kind of sameness that is quite different. This is the sense of déjà-vu we experience when something looks familiar. A mountain switchback is when you notice similar vistas, but from a different perspective. Throughout our journeys, common themes pop up such as betrayal, renewal, career change, discouragement, anticipation, forgiveness, weariness, confusion, and peace. "I feel like I've been here before" and "Here we go again" are common thoughts during these times. "Why does this look strangely familiar?"

Familiarity may cause self-doubt, making us think we're not really progressing, but just going in circles. Going through a challenge doesn't mean we won't visit it again. But when we're progressing, the perspective changes. We curse the difficult times less, embracing them for what they are. Our blaming God decreases as we accept conditions faster. This is SI at its finest. We fret less. As a result, our response reduces the stress of those around us. The same circumstance would have thrown us for a loop in the past. But now we're more at ease. Growth conditions cycle, like seasons in the year. What changes is your response as you progress.

Reward Progress

A common error we make on our journey is comparing ourselves with others. Family-of-origin issues, chemical imbalances, and any number of other dents we pick up along the way make our progress more difficult than others who may be fortunate enough to avoid these challenges. Comparing our outsides with someone else's insides is a self-defeating practice. We can never be sure what someone else has endured to get them where they are today.

Our goal is to celebrate victories, both small and large. When you see someone else progress, tell him. Let him know you noticed a change in his attitude or actions. This is the power of a Travel Team: you're able to witness the others' growth and earn the right to speak into their lives.

The strongest human motivator is rewarding desired behavior. Outside of a Travel Team, people rarely know you well. They are unaware of your growth and development. They seldom tune in to your recent battles and turmoil. But when people become aware of each other's growth, their responsibility is to affirm the improvement.

"Hey, Jesse, I really liked the way you handled that situation on the court today. You kept your cool. Nice job."

"Angela, just wanted to let you know that I noticed how well you seem to be dealing with your ex. Hang in there."

"Jeff, congrats on the promotion. Way to persevere through some pretty difficult conditions at work."

"Suzi, one hundred days sober. Way to go, girl! Proud of you."

Kudos like these become a big deal as we affirm someone's growth. The Bible is filled with celebrations, holidays (Holy Days), and commemoratives.

Interaction Ideas:

1. What is one thing you got out of this chapter?

2. What's a faux fruit you've experienced in someone that disappointed you? If you're gutsy, what's a faux fruit you've noticed in yourself at times?

3. Describe a person you know well and admire, who exhibits high SI.

4. List various people or roles in your life that may provide angles toward a 360-degree perspective (e.g., employees, family members, etc.).

Activity: If you're in a living room, café, or seated around a table, have everyone do a brief sketch of the room from their angle. Do this for five minutes or until most have a rough draft. Then compare and contrast everyone's paper. You're all sitting in the same room, but you see different things depending on where you're sitting. How is this similar to gaining various perspectives on our own lives?

NINE

Roadblocks and Detours

How to Stay Out of the Ditch

While living in Scottsdale, friends and I would occasionally climb Camelback Mountain, a beautiful, natural, sandstone monument in the middle of the city. Sometimes while we grunted and groaned up the steep passages, gazelle-types sprinted by us, seemingly unencumbered by weight and gravity. Their lean, low-body-fat physiques put them in a different category than the rest of us. I'd turn to my colleagues inching up the trail and mutter, "Amazing, isn't it?"

People increase their SI at varying rates and rarely consistently. Even with the right methods, we may experience periods of no or low growth, followed by a period yielding tremendous growth. Like physical development during childhood and adolescence, we improve spiritually in spurts, followed by times of slow growth. But over the long haul, a healthy soul will naturally progress, if implementing proper SI methods. Spiritual fruit becomes more evident as we deepen in character and faith. Maturity becomes a realistic expectation.

But even with the proper methods, we can run into invisible barriers that seem to prevent us from progressing as we have been. Think of a garden hose. You turn the water on at the valve, but if when you squeeze the nozzle handle, only a trickle dribbles out, chances are there's a kink in your hose. Soul kinks impede the flow of God in our lives that in turn reduce the amount and rate of growth.

The naive suggest that the only thing you need for soul growth is motivation. "If you really wanted to grow, you would," implying sincerity is king. Although commitment certainly is a factor, it is not the silver-bullet solution. Many well-intended, sincere, and committed people languish under the burden of such shoddy advice. "Believe, you just need to believe more." We end up turning natural soul growth into a me-not-God process. After running into so many spiritual cul-de-sacs, many give up, concluding that soul growth simply isn't for them. Many abandon faith altogether or settle for a lackluster spiritual life. Most lower their expectations significantly so they no longer feel disappointed with the results.

There are common reasons for hitting these glasslike barriers in our journey, even when implementing the right SI methods. Certain inhibitors decrease our speed and can thwart growth altogether. Following are seven common roadblocks I've observed in working with people, along with a simple detour to help you avoid getting stuck.

Toxic Faith

A person's experience is often influenced by the religious attitudes and actions of others, as well as theological teaching. As Mark Twain said, "A cat won't sit on a hot stove, after doing it once. Of course, he won't sit on a cold stove either." Interacting with religious zealots exhibiting low SI can result in an aversion to faith. Normal people are turned off by judgmental, condemning, self-righteous attitudes. When these are exhibited by people claiming to follow Jesus, it only fits that they'd have little interest in pursuing God, thus guilt by association. Psychology 101 students recognize this as a simple stimulus response connection. The negative traits of low SI may be the most significant reason that people in general are not turned on to following Jesus. They resist faith based on their interactions with those lacking spiritual intelligence.

Also, when a person with faith whom we admire betrays or lets us down, this failure can impact us negatively. Right or wrong, people often are targets of our faith. A person's success or failure in the pursuit of God can detour others from pursuing theirs.

Two of my friends are guys who've pretty much given up on God. They both shared similar immersions into conservative, evangelical faith. One became a mover and shaker among a top-level group of televangelists. His eyewitness tales of Madison Avenue–caliber fundraising campaigns, jetting to crusades, and backstage shenanigans are both riveting and shocking. The other friend was fluent in the Christian music industry and then got tangled in a pretty legalistic community of zealots. While the theology of these guys seemed grounded on an intellectual level, their interaction with unhealthy leaders, respected and emulated by an adoring following, left them disillusioned.

Having been a pastor for twenty years and the executive editor of a national magazine for pastors, I've had the opportunity to interact with a lot of pastors and church leaders over the years. I've met a growing number of seasoned veterans, mostly current or former pastors, who wrestle with their own doubts and suspicions. I'm convinced, as are many of them, that this has little or nothing to do with Jesus or his teachings. Rather, it is about getting caught in the machinery of church, programs, politics, and the dark side of both parishioners and colleagues who we hope would exhibit maturity, but for whatever reason, do not. A side effect of low-grade SI is the tainting of the perceived Jesus who in reality has the ability to elevate us beyond these characteristics that repulse us.

Detour: The difficulty of growing out of toxic faith is that although SI helps us distinguish faith in people versus faith in God, toxic faith prevents us from obtaining SI. The best antidote is finding a person with high SI to model and clarify what is healthy theology and help us work through our disappointments with those lacking SI, but appearing faith-filled.

Family-of-Origin Issues

A few years ago, while wrestling with some midlife transition issues, I sought the help of a group of professional counselors. Through this intervention, I was able to identify experiences in my past that shaped me as an adult. Unfortunately, pride and ignorance prevented me from seeking help sooner. I believe every pastor, priest, and rabbi should be required to go through a battery of assessments and counseling sessions before becoming an official spiritual leader. The results would transform many. I'm embarrassed to think how my family and ministry life would have improved had I unpacked my baggage earlier.

I came to understand how dysfunctions in my childhood home helped create residual issues that later impacted my relationships and ministry. While it's easy to dismiss childhood experiences as blaming, there is a big difference between acknowledging influences in our lives while we're moldable and avoiding responsibility for our actions. One of the primary motivators for my work in developing a leadership training program for preteens through KidLead was to give young leaders a head start that I wish I had.

I can think of scores of people I've met whose family-of-origin issues created spiritual barriers. One example was a woman in our church who won beauty pageants, but battled alcohol abuse and went through two unsuccessful marriages, heading for a third before the age of forty. Her roller-coaster faith made people wonder where she might be in her spiritual journey on any given week. Frequent tears of sincerity conveyed her desire to love God and make right decisions, but mangled scars from her childhood continued to limit her ability to embrace the life she so desperately sought.

All of us have a degree of family-of-origin issues that impact us. For some, there are the scars of abandonment, resulting from a nasty divorce or lack of parental presence altogether. For others there are the present wounds of past sexual abuse. The power of an adult in the life of a child can be seen in any number of individual hurts, accumulating as social pathologies. Damaged self-esteem and identity issues naturally intersect with the spiritual, when we are instructed to believe in a good God who is in control and who desires to relate to us as a heavenly parent.

Detour: Many of these sins of others are significant enough to limit our SI. No matter how much we pray, read the Bible, or attend religious events, we'll be thwarted unless we also pursue professional emotional help. Therapists, like any help provider, should be interviewed, screened, and vetted to increase the chances of effective counseling.

Low EI

In addition to family-of-origin issues, there are other emotional matters that can impede our spiritual growth. Confusion exists in faith communities as to what it means to be mature and how spiritual growth is influenced by our psychological development. People with low emotional intelligence will find it more difficult to mature spiritually than those with high EI. Spiritual maturity is connected to psychological development. Much of what pastors strive to do spiritually is directly related to what psychologists and counselors try to accomplish through their means.

Jack was one of those die-hard, highly committed guys who'd do anything he could to help you. But Jack was socially awkward. He'd say and do things that would scare those who did not understand him. As a result, he had a difficult time making friends. Jack was faithful in serving and in attending worship services, Bible studies, and retreats. While he grew significantly, he also continued to struggle in areas directly related to his emotional intelligence. In his case, his low emotional intelligence had a direct connection with his SI.

Our oldest son, Jeff, is pursuing doctoral work in the area of how psychology and theology interact. The connection of these two fields is obvious when you look at the characteristics of SI. The more we're able to learn about how these realms overlap, the better equipped we'll be to assist people in acquiring SI.

Detour: Again, consider finding a quality, professional therapist to help you unpack issues that may be impeding your progress spiritually. Chemical issues can be addressed with minor medication. Other solutions can address post-traumatic syndrome and any number of neuroses. The best combination is for spiritual guides and therapists to work together, helping us make these connections in our lives.

Diminutive Right Brain

While I'm teaching beyond my expertise at this point, I believe that certain people struggle with issues that are neurological in nature. Some neuroscience research suggests that brain synapses prevent some people from experiencing spiritual growth because they have limited capacity in their right hemisphere. Faith is predominately a right-brain function, meaning that we come to our understanding of God and spiritual things primarily out of a right hemispheric region.

One guy I got to know, Bill, was incredibly intelligent, a brilliant engineer in the medical field. He may have been borderline genius, but nearly everything he struggled with seemed to be in the area of trusting the unseen. Bill could not attribute certain events in the Bible and in people's lives to God. He thought this was a cop-out, the rationale of the ignorant to explain things they could not understand. Bill's wife acknowledged his lack of emotional involvement in their marriage, even though they both loved each other. While Bill had faith and invested a lot of time and energy into his spiritual life, his glass ceiling seemed to be connected to an inability to process things in his right hemisphere, recognized as the seat of faith, emotions, creativity, and spirituality.

Detour: While training and medication can increase right-brain functions, a person's inability to interact with certain brain areas can detour his or her path toward SI. Again, a person with this condition can possess faith, but perhaps not to the point of spiritual maturity. Faith is dwarfed and will never fully develop.

Control Issues

Control issues are generally results of fear. When we are afraid, we tend to pursue situations that limit risks and re-duce unknowns. When a person has a need to control life or environment, SI is reduced, because faith is a matter of transferring personal control to God. Those in the recovery movement understand the idea of letting go and trusting a "higher power" for what they do not understand and cannot control. SI requires the same act of surrendering control. When a person is unable or unwilling to let go, this will affect his or her SI. Whether it's a type A, high-powered CEO, or a worrisome accountant, control issues can negatively impact our pursuit of maturity.

Bob was a former fighter pilot who began a relationship with God in our church. Wherever Bob went, he'd create conflict because he tried to manhandle everything and ended up offending people who had much opportunity to interact with him in a task or endeavor. Bob just couldn't let go. He had to try to take charge. This overflowed into his spiritual walk too. Although Bob grew significantly, he seemed to hit a plateau that never yielded the sort of spiritual fruit that one might expect from a Jesus-follower. He could not seem to let go in his journey with God. Bob's need to be in charge of his life prevented him from experiencing the sort of attitudes and actions characteristic of high SI.

Detour: The solution is often a matter of confronting or being confronted by others and forming an alliance with those who struggle in this area. Acute cases would benefit from professional therapy.

Narcissism

Self-centered people have a difficult time acquiring SI. The greatest gift of faith may be the empowerment to get beyond ourselves. As Rick Warren begins in his book *The Purpose Driven Life*, "It's not about you." The power of a Travel Team and Experiencing the Trip together is that you begin to discover how selfish you are. Working with others through their experiences and then serving people less fortunate (or at times more fortunate) than you, are behavioral ways of breaking out of the black hole of self-interest.

When I think of narcissism, one person that comes to mind is Carol. She was a charismatic leader, a magnet for getting attention in a social setting. Her expertise for style and grooming meant that she always looked like a million bucks. It also led to an inordinate number of plastic surgeries and a lot of people who embraced her at a superficial level but never really felt like they knew her below the surface. Carol seemed to be stuck on Carol and no amount of budging or life trauma seemed sufficient to move her out of her self-orbit. While we may glibly suggest that the nature of sin itself is self-centeredness, narcissism is a niche in this category. The result is an inability to acquire SI, in spite of heroic efforts.

Detour: One of the best means of counteracting the temptation of self-centeredness is voluntarily engaging in situations that require serving others. Whether it's feeding the homeless, serving an unwed mothers' facility, or fixing up an orphanage, denying yourself for the sake of others is an external means of producing internal growth.

Spiritual Oppression

A seventh SI inhibitor may seem somewhat mystical and extreme for some, even sci-fi sounding, but it is very evident in various third-world cultures. This is the influence of spiritual oppression. In certain subcultures, the spiritual realm is more active or at least more observable than in others. Historically, there are accounts of evil spirits, witchcraft, and sorcery, which should be considered as possible inhibitors, even in our culture.

A friend of mine, Tim Elmore, has had a number of experiences with people who clearly had spiritual struggles that transcended the emotional and physical realms. I use Tim as an example because he's not one of those scary, sees-a-demon-behind-every-bush kind of guys. As you hear him recount episodes of confronting evil spirits in a troubled person who came to him for help, you recognize that the realm beyond what is visible is very real and complex. Examples of observable, paranormal activities related to the spiritual realm include speaking in strange and multiple voices, bursting with exceptional strength, and seeing objects moving on their own.

Detour: The antidote to this is strategic intercessory prayer and the help of someone gifted in a deliverance ministry. This is usually a special calling and skill set.

Seeking Assistance

Because several of these healing detours suggest professional counseling, let me provide some ideas for finding an effective counselor. Most people are haphazard when they seek a counselor, leading to expensive and frustrating results.

1. If a challenge you battle is depression, negativity, or anger, you may want to have an appropriate panel of blood work done, informing your medical doctor about your concerns. Sometimes, people go through long-term therapy when their challenge is actually a chemical imbalance that can be significantly improved with appropriate medications. Consider taking this step first.
2. Ask a pastor, trusted friend, or other confidant who is apt to know more than one counselor, who can recommend a couple names for contact. This certainly beats the yellow pages, Internet, or cold calling.
3. Interview the counselor before you begin counseling, much like you would before hiring an employee or consultant. This person is working for you, to coach you through some challenging processes. Ask the counselor about his or her specialties, since a degree in psychology does not make one an authority in all areas. If a person specializes in divorce recovery and your perceived need is with fear, move on. Then, if you are able, verbalize what you perceive the problem is that you want to address. Discuss openly your interest in spiritual growth and faith and ask the counselor to share his or her views on this subject as well. Similar beliefs do not mean you've found a good counselor, but dissimilar beliefs will often frustrate the situation as it relates to SI.
4. Discuss cost factors. Counseling can be an expensive healing venture. See if your health insurance covers counseling and how much. If finances are tight, ask the counselor if he or she has a sliding fee scale, based on a client's ability to pay. You may be able to compromise by spreading out the counseling sessions or use groups versus one-on-one counseling.

5. Look for some sort of measurable progress in ninety days. Do not confuse this with total healing, but rather a synchronized compatibility regarding style and technique. One size does not fit all. Every counselor has a limited range of styles and techniques that he or she employs in a counseling process. When there is a mismatch in terms of what the counselor believes works versus what your challenge requires, then progress will be very slow and perhaps nonexistent. Counselors are human too. They have bills to pay and may feel they can help a person, whether or not they can. When one person makes a living from the problems of another, there is a professional challenge of knowing when it is best to recommend another counselor or to end sessions. While three months is rarely the conclusion of effective counseling, it should be the approximate milestone for sensing whether or not the counseling is being effective.

Summary

When Jesus and the learners came in contact with a blind man, the learners asked Jesus whose sin had caused the blindness (John 9:1–3). Jesus said it was not the result of sin. Just as physical disabilities can challenge your progress in life, emotional and spiritual issues can challenge your journey toward maturity. Unspiritual factors can thwart SI, even if you're using Jesus's methods. As you address these, you can improve your rate of progress. These influences listed should be considered if you strive to apply the methods outlined in this book for at least two years, and yet see minimal results. This is a sign that one or more of these inhibitors are likely decreasing your success. As you address them, you should see accelerated growth toward maturity.

Interaction Ideas:

1. What is one thing you got out of this chapter?

2. Of the various blockages noted, which one might be troubling someone whom you know well?

3. Discuss your thoughts on the relationship between spiritual and emotional intelligence.

4. How do you think family-of-origin matters can thwart spiritual growth?

Activity: Write differing amounts of money on slips of paper, one for each person in your group. Keep the amounts between fifty cents and five dollars, but different. Instruct everyone to take out a slip of paper and hold it without looking at it until everyone has one. "Your job is to give the person on your right the amount of money on your slip of paper. You can either give it now, take it off the person's bill if you're at a restaurant, or pay him or her next time you meet."

After everyone opens their IOUs, talk about why at times life is random and the burdens we carry are not necessarily ones that we created. How are some of these soul growth barriers self-induced and how might some of them be burdens from birth (luck of the draw)?

TEN

Makes and Models

Determining Your Soul Type

Although spiritual intelligence is available to everyone, it will look somewhat different from person to person. One reason for this is soul types, a basic spiritual wiring affecting how we relate to God and pursue growth. I'm convinced that certain types of churches attract certain collective groups of psychographics. For example, demonstratively charismatic and Pentecostal groups draw a similar style of person with a flair for the dramatic and inclination toward the super-natural. Contemplatives are inclined to attend more reserved worship styles, common in Catholic and mainline congregations. There's a certain mind set drawn toward independent, fundamentalist churches, as well as Bible churches. Birds of a feather do flock together, each leaning toward believing that his preferred style is better than others. But soul types can be found in each of these psychographic groups.

While personality temperaments also affect our spiritual path, soul typology is a different, other layer of our complexity. Many people never pursue SI because they've come to believe they're less spiritual by nature. When typical religious programs fail to turn their crank, they conclude soul growth

163

isn't for them. Confusing the organizational church with God, they assume that their soul just isn't programmed for spiritual growth the same as others.

While they may be happy for friends or family members who seem quite satisfied, conventional soul growth means don't seem to work for them. Because of this, they either are laden with guilt, wondering what's wrong with them, or they just give up hoping for a deep connection with God altogether.

Over the years, I've noticed five dominant soul types: Pure Soul, Rebel, Pragmatist, Evangelist, and Cyclist. Like personality types, each possesses unique strengths and weaknesses. Knowing what type you are can aid in your being more gracious toward others, as well as not comparing or demeaning the way you're wired. Perhaps the most significant impact is motivation. By recognizing that soul types exist, those without a stereotypical bend for piety and formal religiosity are energized to pursue SI, but through different means than their more religious friends. Following are brief descriptions of each.

The Pure Soul

My wife, Nancy, is a pure soul. While she'd never claim to be, or even be comfortable being called this, she just seems to have a natural God-connection. She's the first to suggest prayer for family situations, is consistent in reading her Bible, and feels truly burdened for those lost in their spiritual journeys and who seem disconnected from God. We have two other close family friends who exude this kind of attitude. One has been a missionary in South Africa most of his life, until being promoted to a leadership role in his mission organization. The other leads a nonprofit focused on mentoring young adult leaders. These Pure Souls are truly humble and self-sacrificing. When you finish a conversation with them, you don't feel guilty, but you do feel as though you've been with someone who thinks they are one of God's favorites.

Some people seem to possess a natural connection to God. Episodes of doubt and rebellion rarely derail them. Their hardwiring brings them back to faith and carries them through temptations of abandoning soul growth. Pure Souls are often churchgoers, but occasionally they are not. The Pure Soul feels comfortable praying regularly, attending Bible studies, and conversing about what God is doing in his or her life. God-talk rolls off her tongue. She initiates conversations on morality, ethics, and ministry. A healthy Pure Soul makes people around her think, "I wonder how I could be more like that. I wish I were as committed as she is."

Unhealthy, religious zealots attempt to appear as Pure Souls, overcompensating for unresolved issues. The result is a judgmental, legalistic, and preachy attitude. After being around one of these, you feel guilty, condemned, and dirty. Healthy Pure Souls have the opposite effect, causing you to admire, desire, and yearn for deeper spirituality. It's similar to the difference between Jesus and the Pharisees.

Pure Souls tend to pursue spiritual disciplines more naturally, not necessarily because they are holier, but since their lives are less cluttered with unspiritual distractions. They can unintentionally discourage people who admire the Pure Soul but feel they could never measure up to that level of spirituality. Understanding soul types helps the Pure Soul not be as disappointed in others when they do not seem to exhibit the same level of zeal.

If you are a Pure Soul, realize that the way you relate to God and the comparative ease by which you prioritize spiritual discussions is not the norm and does not automatically result in high SI. You may be blessed with greater clarity and more natural inclination to pursue the things of God, but others are not necessarily more carnal just because they are not wired the same. By realizing this, you can avoid looking down on those who seem less pious. While intimidation is not your intent, grace-giving will help those with different soul types to feel more secure around you.

Characteristics:

- Excels in pure motives
- Is self-motivated to pray and read the Bible
- Is passionate about spiritual things
- Frequently pursues God through more organized means

Pursuing SI:

- Augment your formal religious practices with SI methods.
- Continue practicing spiritual disciplines.
- Be aware that you can be intimidating; try not to project a holier-than-thou attitude.

The Evangelist

Chad is a salesman by nature, and that spills over into the way he talks about God and expresses his spiritual journey. He's enthusiastic, but you don't get the feeling that he's being fake or manipulative. Chad can just as easily talk about baseball, the latest news event, or a Bible passage he read that morning, but he does them all with a sense of optimism and energy. Chad is a classic Evangelist.

The Evangelist, in the sense that we're using the label, is a person who has a psychographic wiring to be very zealous with what he or she believes. Evangelists are like Pure Souls on steroids. They tend to enjoy more dramatic church services, televangelist crusades, and emotionally laden God-sightings. The strength of the Evangelist is fervor and passion. The weakness is shallowness and emotionalism, flitting from one spiritual celebrity to another and criticizing others for not sharing the same enthusiasm.

The Evangelist is easily preoccupied with religious entertainment, confusing participation with significant soul growth. SI is not what we say or how we talk, but is demonstrated in how we live and exhibit authentic qualities of maturity. Evangelists run the risk of offending people who are not like them and who do not telegraph the same passion they feel. They alienate themselves from others because they can be verbose, equating enthusiasm with spirituality. Evangelists do well to recognize their soul type and make sure that exciting, formal soul growth events are not substitutes for implementing the methods Jesus used. Mass gatherings can energize the soul, but they rarely result in significant SI.

If you are an Evangelist, be conscious of your tendency to intimidate and alienate those who do not share the type of passion you exude. Others are not necessarily less spiritual. If your soul type is not an Evangelist, be aware that when you're around one or more, their zeal can be authentic and not feigned. They do not necessarily have more or less SI than you; your natural wirings are primarily different.

Characteristics:

- Expresses passion and verbal zeal for spiritual things
- Tends to pursue dynamic meetings that are often emotionally stimulating
- Can knowingly or unknowingly intimidate others with zeal
- Sometimes places too much emphasis on formal events instead of Jesus's methods

Pursuing SI:

- Find others with your soul type and implement Jesus's soul growth methods as you enjoy other settings.
- Develop a practical discipline that helps you apply what you learn and feel.

- Be conscious that you can be intimidating; try not to project a holier-than-thou attitude in your speech and emotions.

The Pragmatist

Bill and Leigh are a very sharp yet extremely humble couple we got to know in Arizona. They are highly involved in community work and consistently open their home for social gatherings, youth events, and meetings as needs arise. They let people use their cabin in Mammoth, where our family has created numerous memories on getaways. Yet Bill and Leigh don't seem overly spiritual in terms of how they express their faith. They don't randomly toss out God-talk, and they appear to be somewhat low-key in their religious experience, especially compared to an Evangelist or even a Pure Soul. Yet, Bill and Leigh exude many of the symptoms of SI. That is because their soul type is that of the Pragmatist.

At the heart of the Pragmatist is a person who is intent on doing good deeds, living the Golden Rule, and treating others with respect. Pragmatists tend to be humble, living lives of service without fanfare or calling attention to themselves, and not making others feel badly for not participating. The difference between a Pragmatist and a moral or ethical person is that the former views his good deeds and neighborly actions as a form of worship, of living the way God wants him to live. The Pragmatist is not inclined to do a lot of philosophizing, studying, or God-talk. Rather, he likes living his faith and getting his hands dirty in helping others, placing far more emphasis on applying Directions than studying and discussing them. But again, don't confuse a humanist trying to do good on his own with a Pragmatist who is spiritually inclined.

Pragmatists can grow weary of Pure Souls and religious types, who in their minds get caught up in religious activities instead of making them tangible. "Too much talk; too little action" is the criticism. A weakness of the Pragmatist is doing too much on his or her own strength and not enough as a result of being in tune with God. It's difficult arguing with a Pragmatist, though, because he or she tries living according to his or her beliefs that are centered around God.

Pragmatists do well gathering with their own soul types, but also enlisting the help of a Path Finder, who can assist them in discovering Directions. The power of a Travel Team is that the Pragmatist can emphasize Experiencing the Trip, whether it is serving in a homeless shelter or being a part of a civic group that benefits others.

Characteristics:

- Focuses on living out faith through acts of service and ethical standards
- Prefers to practice more than preach
- Is often humble, quietly doing good as a means of reflecting faith in God
- Can get sidelined in formal religious services and turned off by talking about faith

Pursuing SI:

- Find others with your soul type in order to share experiences in serving.
- Pursue a Path Finder who might introduce Directions for discussion that add depth to your life.
- Avoid being irritated by those who are more zealous in formal spiritual pursuits.

The Rebel

Phil is quite famous in certain circles, which is why I'm not using his real name. He's an incredibly talented strategist and brilliant author. But he's also somewhat critical of business-as-usual in the traditional local church. For a while, Phil's "church" consisted of Sunday mornings at the beach, reading Scriptures and meditating, while his wife and girls attended a nearby church. Later, Phil began joining his family at a house church. Because of Phil's reputation in the Christian realm, he's often criticized for his views that are nontraditional and that seem to joust with commonly accepted practices. But when you spend time with Phil, you get to know quite a different person. You perceive his connection with God and sincere burden for the church. Phil is a Rebel. In fact, a growing number of catalysts for change in recent years, some of whom have become famous authors and speakers in U.S. Christianity, are Rebels.

People interested in God and spiritual things, but who do not feel like they fit into church or more traditional soul growth programs, may be Rebels. Rebels are not anti-God or spiritually apathetic, but they do feel constrained by religious norms and push back on the way things are done. This causes others to label them as troublemakers, disobedient, and immature. Such labeling can demotivate the Rebel by making him believe he's less spiritual, too worldly, and even cause him to give up pursuing God. Undoubtedly, some of the prophets of the Old Testament were Pure Souls, but some were likely Rebels.

God created the Rebel soul. Sometimes in Scripture, we can see Rebel tendencies in Jesus as he pushed back on religious tradition, worn paths to God, and socially accepted God-talk of his day. While we can also see the Pure Soul in Jesus, we find situations where Jesus bucked the system and went his own way, undeterred by those pressing him to conform. Unfortunately, most organized spiritual activities are not Rebel-friendly; they are flawed in how they understand and relate to the Rebel soul.

Rebels may attend church in order to appease a spouse, friend, or family member with a different soul type, but they are only mildly engaged at best, discouraged because they assume this is the only means to SI. As a result, they often end up feeling that God isn't for them. They don't have anything against God personally, but because they equate the Pure Soul and systematized spiritual activities with godliness, anything else seems unspiritual. They may go through the motions, but they remain unfulfilled and noncommittal, and they fail to mature. Like the stereotypical ugly stepchild, they feel left out, slighted, and that their heavenly Parent doesn't love them as much as others.

The free spirit of the Rebel intuitively rejects systematized means of soul growth. Unfortunately, the undisciplined Rebel may bounce around with no plan at all. Fearful of getting stuck in a rut, the Rebel often goes too far the other way and embraces a lifestyle that is ineffective for spiritual growth. The result is diminished SI. But the Rebel can acquire spiritual intelligence through means that look quite different and seem counterintuitive to the Pure Soul. Rebels may want to gather with other Rebels on their Travel Team and play around with a variety of formats that keep their interest, avoiding the trappings of more traditional soul growth strategies.

Characteristics:

- Is resistant to traditional religious programs and services
- Believes that God speaks through real-life situations more than "holy" venues
- Recognizes the need for spiritual growth, but often feels unfulfilled when trying
- Conveys a good heart wrapped up in rough edges

Pursuing SI:

- Find others with your soul type to intentionally journey together spiritually.

- Develop challenging but creative means, since you're not apt to find them on bookstore shelves, Christian television, or in most churches.
- Be honest about separating what does not fit traditional means with what is truly detrimental to your soul growth.

The Cyclist

I was raised in a pretty traditional, conservative church. The older I got, the less I felt in touch with the formalities. As my wife and I began sensing God leading us to begin a church, we decided to launch one that was not necessarily conventional, but was more in line with the one we'd like to attend ourselves. Approximately two-thirds of the attendees in our two church starts had either abandoned traditional church or had no previous church experience. And still, in the midst of both of those projects, I experienced periods when my soul wandered. Although I was providing spiritual growth resources for those in our congregation, I yearned for more mystical, contemplative means as reflected in the early desert fathers. I found myself drawn toward monasteries and retreat centers. It was during one of these journeys that I wrote my book on brokenness. While we currently attend a large church where my wife is on staff, I could take or leave a formal church experience, contemporary or not. I am satisfied with the sole community of a Travel Team "doing life" together. During my first couple of inner transitions, I was worried that I might be a spiritual schizophrenic. I felt concerned that one style didn't seem to fit me the entire journey. But I've come to realize that my soul type is that of a Cyclist.

The Cyclist is akin to the Rebel, in that more traditional, formal means don't always work for him; he is different in that sometimes they do. The Cyclist appears to have a variety of soul types—his appetite changes. This seasonality is in and of itself a characteristic of who he is spiritually. The Cyclist can't necessarily predict how long these seasons will last. For some, a preferred style may seem to work for years. For others, it's a matter of months. For example, a person for whom a liturgical church "has worked" finds herself seeking a faith community that is far more emotive and relevant. A person who has enjoyed a megachurch begins yearning for the organic qualities of a house church.

A Cyclist is different than a person lacking SI who is up and down, influenced heavily by each new religious trend and guru. When a Cyclist is in the midst of changing a spiritual growth preference, she can confuse these feelings with apathy for God, when in reality it is more a boredom with the current style of soul growth. The Cyclist experiences more of a seasonal growth pattern. Instead of consistent, gradual maturation, the Cyclist goes through rhythmic phases and patterns that occur over and over.

A Cyclist soul type, similar to a Rebel, needs to be in tune with what is and isn't working in his life spiritually. But unlike the Rebel, who may never feel at home in a more traditional and organized soul growth venue, the Cyclist may find that she needs more formal means such as church, or a community Bible study, or service roles. Then may come a season when that doesn't seem to work, so that a different style worship service, church, or ministry role is required to keep the soul engaged in growth and development.

The difference between a Cyclist's growth pattern and someone who is merely flaky, noncommittal, or flighty, is that the Cyclist is growing and the other person is avoiding growth for fear of going too deep in relationships, or of working through the hard things that are preventing SI.

A Cyclist does well to connect with other Cyclists, but may find this difficult in that at any given time, a Cyclist appears to be another soul type. As Cyclists bond with each other and then feel themselves needing something different, they are prone to either question their own spirituality or sense others thinking that, causing them to further question themselves.

Characteristics:

- Is open to more than one style of soul growth
- Must pursue other formats when what worked for a while may fade
- Preferences vary in time, often defying any logical reason
- May confuse boredom of a certain style of soul growth with spiritual apathy, creating self-doubt

Pursuing SI:

- Find others with your soul type and share your current journey with these people in a Travel Team.
- Become familiar with a variety of ancillary spiritual venues so that you can pursue these when one begins to lose its effectiveness with you.
- Do not give up on God when transitioning to a different style of worship or spiritual practice.

The discussion of soul types may seem a bit odd for people who tend to be locked in to a certain model of how spiritual growth should take place, sort of a one-size-fits-all. It is also somewhat subjective, because in these limited descriptions, a person may find it difficult to confidently identify with any one. The purpose of this chapter is not so much to create a new paradigm of spirituality. Rather, it is to help us recognize that a variety of spiritual wirings exist, and the way we approach God and soul growth is affected by them. The goal is not to be intimidated by those who typically are perceived to be more spiritual, when really they are not. Jesus's method for soul growth will work for you, but the way you go about using that method may look different than others.

Interaction Ideas:

1. What is one thing you got out of this chapter?

2. Which of these soul types did you relate to most?

3. Describe people who came to mind for the other categories.

4. Why is it helpful to consider different soul types, rather than thinking that everyone is the same in this area?

Activity: Provide a plate with different types of cookies and encourage each person to take a bite of each type. (You can do this with other food categories such as vegetables, drinks, chips, or fruits.) Ask the group to describe the various tastes, textures, and preferences. Discuss why it is not better or worse to have a certain soul type and why comparing ours with someone else's can be unhealthy.

ELEVEN

Enjoying the Journey

Spiritual Intelligence Is Wings Not Weights

My sons, like most kids, are not too fond of road trips. But my wife and I have learned that it doesn't take much to spice up the drive, whether it's an ice cream stop, playing catch in the parking lot, or family games to pass the time. Because soul growth is just as much journey as arrival, it might be helpful to know how we grow along the way. By better understanding this, we can lower our frustration level and raise the joy factor.

The Difference between Fullness and Capacity

One thing that helps us understand soul growth is the difference between being full of God and increasing our spiritual capacity. If you have a twenty-four-ounce drink cup and you fill it to the brim, you have twenty-four ounces of beverage. But if you're really thirsty, you go for a forty-four-ounce container. When it's full, you've got forty-four ounces of beverage. The concept isn't rocket science. But it does help explain the difference between being fully committed to knowing Jesus and real maturity. Fullness marks the amount of you that God has. Capacity has to do with the amount of God you have in terms of maturity. Fullness is about commitment, intent, and mode of living. Capacity is about strength, wisdom, and depth of living.

Both fullness and capacity have to do with soul purity and relying on God. Both are equal in value in terms of loving God. But capacity helps us understand why some people are able to respond spiritually to seemingly unimaginable odds, while others buckle quickly. Shallow harbors only allow certain-sized sailing vessels, whereas deep harbors can handle all sizes of ships. Spiritual ships, opportunities to do great things for God and seeing God do great things through us, require deep spiritual water.

When our sons were toddlers, we loved their slobbery kisses, funny ways of pronouncing things, and impish hugs. But now, as our sons are fifteen, nineteen, and twenty-one, we'd be concerned if we received the very same expressions of their love. A baby and toddler are indeed fully human, but they have yet to grow to their full capacity. Parents want to know that their child is healthy each step of the way. If a two-year-old is behaving as a two-year-old should, they are content. But when a six-year-old is stuck in a two-year-old mode, parents are justifiably concerned. When a person develops spiritually, there are similar expectations. When you get stuck at a certain capacity, chances are you've not lived for long in God's fullness, because there is a natural progression that increases our ability to retain more and more of God in our lives.

The objective of SI is twofold. We want to keep the flow of God constant and full as well as increase our capacity for God.

God's Methods for Soul Expansion

God is in the people-building business. There are a variety of means that God employs to increase our spiritual capacity.

They can become processes to enjoy and not fear, so long as we know what God's up to. We'll explain three categories by which God accomplishes this.

1. Something neat in something new

Genesis says that God created the world in six days and then rested. But it doesn't say that God stopped creating after the sixth day. Throughout Scripture, God initiates new things. "See, I am doing a new thing! Now it springs up; do you not perceive it? I am making a way in the desert and streams in the wasteland" (Isa. 43:19). The God of the Bible is not a dusty, boring plodder but is vibrant, active, and doing new things left and right. Like a homeowner who wants to add an extra room onto the side of the house, God is interested in expanding the living space within your life. One method is to do new things in your life so that you let go of familiar settings that limit your experiences.

a. The inner move. Sometimes God works quietly, internally, where few people can see what you're learning and where you're growing. At other times, the creating is noisy, evident to all around you. While you may not move physically, your inner world is being rearranged. This can happen in various ways.

Spiritual lessons come in many forms. They may be through hearing a message, reading a book, listening to a song, conversing with a friend, or spending time alone with God. The lesson may be one of hope, instruction, or conviction. Spiritual spankings involve corrections that no one enjoys but provide discipline for us to improve our attitudes and actions. Spiritual lessons come in many forms to the person open to them. They may surprise us. Certainly everything is not a spiritual lesson. Beware of those who see them everywhere, for more than likely they've lost a grip on reality. On the other hand, spiritual learnings are a part of our ongoing daily lives, if we develop eyes to see them.

One way to improve the look of your house is to move your furniture. The change interrupts boredom and the monotony that grows like mold on last week's leftovers. God periodically rearranges our internal furniture. It may come externally, such as when a friend moves away, an associate makes a snide remark, or a challenge pops up at work. The surprise effect awakens you. You have not physically moved, but your environment has changed, forcing you to respond. While God does not always initiate these, changes provide opportunities for soul growth in terms of how you respond. They tap spiritual reserves you may not have harnessed in the past.

b. The outer move. Sometimes God expands our soul by changing our physical setting. Whether it's Abram being redirected from Ur, Moses withdrawing from shepherding, Joseph leaving family, Joshua entering the Promised Land, or Peter exiting his fishing career, God has a track record of expanding souls through relocation. Every move we experience may not be God-led. Perhaps we can't hold a job or we're tempestuous in decision making. But open doors can be intentional means of expanding our spiritual capacity. Familiar settings can easily become comfort zones that lull us asleep. Because we are creatures of habit, strategic moves have a way of interrupting our security systems. Forcing us into new relationships, expanding our responsibilities, and leading us to experience faith in the fog are ways that God expands our soul's capacity.

During an unfortunate job termination I experienced a few years ago, our income actually went up as friends and well-wishers donated money to help us get through our transition phase until a new job opened. The difficult experience for our family expanded our faith and helped us realize, in a very tangible and profound way, that our security is in God, not jobs, churches, or people. Out of nowhere we had more than we needed to make it through a potentially frightening period. This uprooting expanded our capacity for God and elevated our trust in future transitions.

2. The hungry heart: Jabez revisited

God's favorite way to expand our soul's capacity comes from our desire to serve and obey him. Years ago, a small book that sold millions of copies focused on the simple prayer of a man named Jabez. "Jabez cried out to the God of Israel, 'Oh, that you would bless me and enlarge my territory! Let your hand be with me, and keep me from harm so that I will be free from pain.' And God granted his request" (1 Chron. 4:10). This type of prayer is an antidote to comfort zones. "God, don't let me settle. May I not be content tomorrow with what I have today." A popular myth suggests you shouldn't ask God to deal with a character issue, or else you'll have to experience pain. "Don't pray for patience, because God will answer your prayers with challenges and bad things." The logic is ludicrous, if you believe God is good. If God has our best in mind, whatever he causes will not be for our harm, but for our gain. While temporarily uncomfortable, these times allow God to increase our capacity by expanding our territories.

"Search me, O God, and know my heart; test me and know my anxious thoughts. See if there is any offensive way in me, and lead me in the way everlasting" (Ps. 139:23–24). Ask God to expand your territory, search your heart, and do something new in your life. If you're honest about getting out of a potential comfort zone, invite God to help you move. Like a good friend with a pickup truck, he'll be there. The path of spiritual intelligence invites God to lead us from the status quo, whether it be to larger territories, new endeavors, or even perseverance in our current zone, comfortable or not.

3. Embracing brokenness

While God's preference is to increase our capacity for him proactively, there are certain lessons we learn best while experiencing difficulties. Brokenness is a term that refers to one's condition during the painful times of life. In my book *Em-*

bracing Brokenness, I talk about this unique spiritual process in more detail. After three years of planting our congregation in the exhaust pipes of Saddleback Church (with Rick Warren), I was nearing burnout and realizing we'd never be the stellar success we'd imagined. I was a part of the Purpose Driven Pastors Conference when it consisted of four guys around Rick's desk, after which we'd break for lunch at the Japanese restaurant next door. The church growth conferences we attended implied that if we did it their way, we too would experience similar results. But even though we'd developed a larger than average core, we realized we'd never be a Saddleback, Mariners, Coast Hills, or Crystal Cathedral. That realization resulted in the death of our dream, leading me on a journey of studying how God grows leaders through times of breaking.

When we experience devastation, trauma, failure, and disconcerting circumstances, part of the purpose is to help us become spiritually pliable, readying us for a deeper view of God. A typical breaking event prompts us to ask, "Why do bad things happen to good people like me?" The more we grow spiritually, we're apt to ask, "Why don't bad things happen to me more?" The more we mature, our sensitivity to our spiritual inadequacies increases.

The bottom line is that you can't always know the cause behind a bad experience. Besides, determining the cause is often not productive. A pastor I know was talking to his children after the September 11, 2001, terrorist attacks on the World Trade Center in New York. He was tempted to tell them that nothing would ever happen to them, that their daddy would keep them safe. He realized this was a lie. He could not guarantee it. His response to his children was this: "You can't always determine how you're going to die or when you're going to die, but you can determine how you will live." Similarly, your response to difficult, painful, "bad" situations is far more important spiritually than knowing the cause or even fixing the problem. A benefit of breaking is realizing that we're not in charge, but God is.

Embracing brokenness means allowing heartbreaks and disappointments to soften, not harden, us. Improper breaking results in bitterness, abandoned faith, and all sorts of emotional damage that hinders relationships. Shrunken souls have less capacity for God. Having pastored for over twenty years, I've met many "walking wounded." These people allowed painful challenges to disrupt their flow of faith.

"And we know that in all things God works for the good of those who love him, who have been called according to his purpose" (Rom. 8:28). Sincere but misled people often quote this verse as a sort of spiritual Band-Aid to heal hurts. Their suggestion is that God caused the painful occurrence to reprove or correct us. Like Job's friends in the Bible, their pious-sounding explanation misses the mark. The above passage says that in all that happens, whether circumstantial, consequential, demonic, or divinely initiated, God has the supernatural ability to create positive from it. He recycles good stuff from garbage. One of the important life lessons for the spiritually intelligent is learning how difficult situations can soften our souls and increase our capacity for God. This understanding will not make the pain go away, but we will no longer feel the need to curse the woe or even explain it. We can embrace our brokenness whether or not we anesthetize the pain or make it go away.

Spiritual Plateaus

Brokenness and God-initiated changes are sometimes needed for us to move out of spiritual comfort zones. Organisms and organizations get to places in their growth where the temptation to remain as they are becomes the dominant theme. During natural life cycles, there are times of growth, rest, harvest, pain, and new growth. Because growth is stressful, we often feel the need for a reprieve. While a short rest may be due, there comes a point when time out becomes a comfort zone, a place where pushing forward does not seem worth the effort. The temptation is to remain in the comfort zone longer than we ought. Too much time in a spiritual rest stop results in stagnation, missed opportunities, pride, blindness, and loss of zeal (Rev. 3:16). Good or bad, God calls us to be pioneers, not settlers.

I used to live north of Denver, Colorado, where I heard this story. Years ago, when Midwest flatlanders began heading west to discover what lay beyond their horizon, they found themselves face-to-face with the fourteen-thousand-foot peaks of the Rocky Mountains. At that point, some of them turned around and went home. Another group decided to settle right where they were—that eventually became the city of Denver. But a small group of explorers were not satisfied with going back or staying put. Instead, they dared to see what was on the other side of the mountains. You need to decide which group you're going to be a part of spiritually. Are you going to go back to the old ways, make camp where you're at, or forge ahead to new territories? My vote is forward.

Here are questions to ask yourself, to see if you may be in a comfort zone:

1. *What new skills have I begun to learn in the last twelve months?* One sign of a comfort zone is that we stay in areas where we've already learned the skills needed to maintain our lives.
2. *Do I plan more than five years in advance?* James chapter two warns us against the pride that can come from firm and long-term planning. This is a way of creating a comfort zone so that we rely on the plan versus our Creator.
3. *Do I plan the future based on my current resources?* God tends to expand our borders and does new things in our lives, requiring different resources and responses.

If you plan based on what you now have, little faith is required.

4. *What new, meaningful relationships have I voluntarily nurtured in the last year?* Spiritual maturity typically requires developing new friendships and new interactions with people, since others help us grow.

5. *When was the last time I sensed God speaking to me? What am I learning right now?* Sensing God's voice in your life and discerning a recent growth instruction pries you from the idea that you're fine the way you are. God does new things to keep us growing.

6. *Who have I introduced to God this year, or who has significantly grown spiritually due to my direct influence? Am I seeing impact from my life in other people?* God's Spirit working through us will change others.

7. *When was the last miracle or "God-thing" I experienced?* God is active, so when we fail to see him working in our lives, it's a sign that we're inactive or straying.

As the saying goes, you can live a thousand days or one day a thousand times. Merely repeating what you've been doing is not the same as progressing. The routine of religious practices can lull us into a sleepy existence that makes us think we're growing when in reality we aren't. Like parents who put inflatable water-wings on their children's arms, confusing them with legitimate floatation devices, a false sense of spiritual security convinces us we're better off then we are.

Keeping the Wineskins Supple

Nancy and I loved going out to dinner with John and Kara. They were a unique couple who seemed to relate to the inner lives of pastors. They were safe. They made us laugh. We always thought of them as a creative and unique pair. But one day, John decided to call it quits and left Kara. Something was going on inside of John that neither I, nor my wife, nor Kara had realized. John was growing cold. Divorce is highest during the first five years of marriage and second highest around midlife. Something happens when you've "been there, done that" and you begin wondering, "Is this as good as it gets?" The issue of boredom and losing one's spark is a matter of spiritual rigor mortis, a hardening of the attitudes that gradually happens over time. The more people I run into, the more I'm convinced there exists a spiritual midlife crisis. You've heard so many sermons, attended countless church events, and become a part of the congregational culture, and you eventually become restless. The same old thing doesn't impress you as it did when you were new in your walk. You lose your fun and spontaneity, becoming stiff and set in your ways.

Jesus said, "[People do not] pour new wine into old wineskins. If they do, the skins will burst, the wine will run out and the wineskins will be ruined. No, they pour new wine into new wineskins, and both are preserved" (Matt. 9:17). In Jesus's day, leather pouches carried fluids. When new, the leather would expand with the gases that new wine produces as it ferments. But after a while, in the arid climate of Palestine, the leather would harden and become inflexible.

The natural tendency in life is to become rigid, inflexible, and lose our pliability—physically, mentally, and spiritually. As the baby boomer generation ages, we're apt to see countless new wrinkle creams and fountain-of-youth remedies flooding the market. But how do you stay spiritually fresh and responsive? How do you maintain a supple soul so that you do not need the involuntary process of breaking? Voluntary brokenness is a means of remaining spiritually receptive, an anti-aging process for the soul, keeping it pliable and responsive to God's leading.

One means of conditioning a flexible soul is through a series of exercises commonly known as spiritual disciplines. Think of these as yoga for the soul. While more exhaustive lists exist, here are five of the most common that seem to be the most practical in terms of normal people applying them on a regular basis.

Seeking: This is another term for praying. Anyone can pray. In fact, national surveys show that a high number of people admit that they do. Someone said as long as there are tests in school, there will be prayer in school. But prayer as a spiritual discipline is more focused and concentrated. It is more like immersing in a hot tub, not just running around in the shower. When combining prayer with one of the other four disciplines, you discover it even more effective. As we mentioned earlier, you may find the exercise of writing in a journal a helpful discipline. If you're like me, sometimes you need help focusing your thoughts and articulating your feelings. Those of us wired to be *doing* something will find this activity helpful when trying to pray. The Psalms are little more than journaled prayers of ancient God-followers.

Solitude: "Very early in the morning, while it was still dark, Jesus got up, left the house and went off to a solitary place, where he prayed" (Mark 1:35). As social beings, we enjoy the presence of others, even as introverts and overstimulated leaders. Solitude is a prolonged time alone with God that allows us to experience new perspective, unadulterated by peer pressure, external interruptions, and distractions. The challenge most of us will battle in solitude is the noise in our heads that does not necessarily disappear with a short drive to the desert, mountains, or ocean. Solitude is more than just a personal vacation. It is a half day to multiday sensory-deprivation event, designed specifically for worship, meditation, and life inspection. While it sounds religiously romantic, most find solitude mildly painful. Boredom and internal noise remind us of how addicted we have become to activities and external pressures that give us a false sense of self-importance.

Study: In this age of sound bytes and information overload, the exercise of spiritual study yields the potential for even greater impact than in less busy eras. Intellectual distractions pull us away from getting good Directions. The goal here is to engage both mind and soul. The emphasis may be a topical study or an involved look at a specific Bible passage or book. The use of modern investigative tools, commentaries, study Bibles, the Internet, word studies, and CD-ROM aids is not just for pastors and theologians. When we engage our intellect and immerse ourselves into specific subjects, God can plow new ground in our lives.

Silence: While silence is obviously adaptable to solitude and prayer exercises, it can also be applied to everyday situations where you consciously increase your listening and decrease your talking. Speech is a significant tool of control. With our conversations we manipulate relationships, broadcast our ideas, and make our presence known. To verbally disappear from society, without going away, is an act of humility. By lowering our self-importance, we stand a better chance of discovering God's importance. A silent retreat is a wonderful experience for a Travel Team, together for a period of time but not interacting. It's a unique twist, being alone in community. While silent, the goal is to hear God better and observe things around us that we filter out as we self-project through speech.

Starving: Giving up something that brings us pleasure is the essence of fasting. The word *starving* is more descriptive of the feeling. The goal of starving is to experience the delay of gratitude that any number of activities bring us, reminding us of how emotionally dependent we become on externals. The common deprivation is food, but an array of desires can be used to create this sense: television, music, sex, shopping, recreation, or specific food items such as soft drinks, desserts, coffee, or bread. Sometimes, starving is good to do when you carry a specific burden. The exercise is not a ploy to manipulate God into answering you, but it is a means of conveying how important something is in your life. "My concern is so heavy that I'm more interested in it than eating or drinking."

While spiritual exercises like these are biblical and have been practiced off and on for centuries, they continue to be contemporary means of keeping our souls limber, reducing the need for breaking. In my one and only golf lesson, the pro explained to me that I was trying to kill the ball when I drove it. "Drive for show, putt for dough" is the golfing slogan. I figured that if I couldn't demonstrate finesse, I'd prove my prowess by killing the ball. But then the pro said, "Let the grip rest in your hand, as if you're about to drop it." That made no sense. How can you cream the ball if you barely hold onto the club? *Oh well, I'll entertain him*, I thought to myself. I eased my white-knuckle grasp of the handle. As lightly as I could, without letting the club float out of my hand, I held on and swung. The ball flew, higher and farther than before. I was amazed.

Hold onto life loosely. Don't grip it too tightly. When we do, we're saying, "It's up to me. I'm in charge of making it happen." But SI says that to go farther in life, we must loosen our grip. Soul exercises, commonly referred to as "spiritual disciplines," help us do that. They are to the soul what yoga and Pilates are to the body, keeping us limber and flexible and holding at bay spiritual rigor mortis. Our capacity for God increases as we let go.

Interaction Ideas:

1. What is one thing you got out of this chapter?

2. Discuss a time when you believe you were being broken.

3. Describe a new thing that required you to grow in a certain area.

4. Discuss whether or not you're on a spiritual plateau right now and why you think that.

5. Which of the spiritual disciplines have you done? How do you do it and what do you get out of doing this?

Activity: Bring in various sizes of water glasses. Clear is best. Have a large, full pitcher of liquid. Let each person pour a certain amount of the liquid in his or her glass. Then discuss further the concept of fullness and capacity, how being full of God is different than capacity for God, and how that relates to maturity.

TWELVE

Are We There Yet?

Recognizing the Destination of Spiritual Intelligence

Where the SI Path Leads

I live near Monterey, California, but our sons go to college in San Diego, nearly seven hours south. For the most part, my wife and I don't mind the drive because we love seeing them as well as San Diego. We enjoy the central coast. Stopping in Santa Barbara is fun. We reminisce about our former homes as we pass Westlake and Mission Viejo. But whether we're coming or going, there's one part of the trip we like the least: the last hour. After about six hours on the road, we're tired.

This book has been a journey and now we've come to the final chapter. You may be tired. When I saw the numerous comments from the editor at this point, I knew I needed to rethink what I was trying to say. One of the best illustrations I've found in counseling is that of knotted fishing string. One thing I learned as a kid when my fishing line got tangled is that sometimes it's better to cut out the knot and start fresh than to try and untangle it. Likewise, in marriage, when there are multiple hurts and miscommunications, sometimes you just need to start fresh—cut the knot and begin anew with your spouse.

So that's what I tried to do in rewriting this chapter: begin fresh.

What I'd like you to know, before we part company, is how to determine your progress. We've talked about measuring growth, getting feedback from others, and checking for signs of maturity, but if you're like me, you're always striving to arrive. "Are we there yet?" "How much farther?"

For the most part, paths and journeys are designed to take us places. So how do you know when you get to SI? Where is "there"? A primary goal of this book is to remove some of the mysticism from soul growth. Far too much effort goes into subjective, esoteric activities void of measurable outcomes. So for a few moments, allow me to paint with some less specific colors to provide a landscape of what we're looking for from the trip.

The journey itself is very much a part of the destination. Hopefully, you'll continue to grow all your life. Saying "nobody's perfect" or "we're constantly arriving" is not necessarily the same as the SI behavitude of humility and growth-seeking. Just yesterday, I was dickering with a fast-food clerk who'd overcharged me for a sandwich. My youngest son suggested that I try to stay calm longer, because the employee didn't understand me. I asked my young coach for more details on how I could improve. After half a century of interacting with people, you'd think I'd get it right, but it was apparent to my fifteen-year-old that I could do better.

Life becomes a perpetual school of improvement, in which you have the opportunity to make the most of everyday interactions with strangers, waiters, impatient commuters, bills, broken pipes, health concerns, and any number of daily events, micro or macro in nature. People with SI acknowledge their need to keep learning. Spiritual maturity is a condition that exhibits qualities reflecting the attitude of Jesus (Phil. 2:3–17).

Destination-itis

My home is near the foothills surrounding Monterey Bay and John Steinbeck's famed Cannery Row. These pastoral hills are dotted with coastal oaks and rock outcroppings. You can find numerous roads providing panoramic views of the scenic shoreline. One drive takes you right along the beach. Another, higher up, overlooks the same area. And yet farther up the hill you can chart a path looking down on the rest. This is much like our journey in spiritual intelligence. Throughout our growth, we'll see the same scenery over and over. The basics in life don't change. But the views differ, based on how far up the hill we've progressed. That means that no matter where we are on our path, we have things we can relate to with others.

Soul growth involves going over many of the same principles again and again, such as faith, holiness, prayer, obedience, and humility, but from different angles, depths, and perspectives. After going through an episode of life learning, you feel like you have it under your belt. "There, I've finally accomplished servanthood." But a few weeks, months, or years later, God reintroduces the topic in your life. Like the mountain path, you look back from time to time at the same vistas, but the view is different because you're at a higher elevation than before.

Jesus embraced paradoxes. If you want to lead, serve; if you want to be first, be last; if you want to live, die. Spiritual intelligence is paradoxical. It is both destination and journey. The path of SI does not necessarily lead us to heaven, or to tangible results such as financial success and physical health. Through it we deepen our connection with God, our Creator, from whom we obtained our spiritual DNA. The longer we stay on the path, the more likely we'll reach our God-given potential to fulfill our call in life and live out our destiny. Understanding that is important to those of us who want something tangible. Working through the concept that being on the path is as much the destination as is arriving, is difficult for many of us who like achievement and finishing projects.

Yet the path is not a treadmill to which you're chained. You can exit anytime you like. Many do. They choose not to progress. Although the motor's running, they stop moving forward. For those of us willing to stay engaged, though, hubris lurks around each corner. Claiming to know more than we do, we're vulnerable to getting stuck. Some set up camps at flat spots in order to rest. Others decide to go back, reversing the trek and losing the growth they have experienced.

SI is about staying on the path and advancing, seeing relationships, work, play, and circumstances from a spiritual perspective, not only physical and emotional ones. Life on this path provides a different way of seeing things, resulting in insights otherwise unobservable. Every metaphor is limited. A footpath is linear, one-dimensional, but soul growth is not. Accomplishing a course of study, ten years of perfect church attendance, and a certificate of ministry are linear, but SI is multidimensional.

Childlike, not Childish

My dad used to warn me about crossing the river on our farm where it appeared shallow, but was in fact deep. Likewise, it can be difficult to accurately assess a person's depth or level of spiritual maturity. There have been times when I've treated a deep person as a shallow one, in part because spiritually intelligent people find little need to let you know they are deep. The opposite is even more common: shallows who fear being perceived as ankle-deep try coming across as "deep wannabes." Jesus often came across as quite simple. But when you're secure in who you are, you don't have to grandstand.

John 14:1–4 says that Jesus knew who he was and from where he'd come. *Then* he got up and washed the feet of his learners. He could do this self-deprecating act of service because his identity and sense of self-worth were not based on what the learners thought of him. Jesus exuded the inner confidence that comes when we are secure in the source of our worth. Knowing who he was, Jesus was able to empty himself and become obedient to death.

SI ultimately results in a transformation of how we think of ourselves. It frees us from the chains of self-centeredness, liberating us to think of others. This increases the likelihood of people showing appreciation for the dignity we give them and respond in kind with honor. SI fulfills us by freeing us from the tyranny of insecurity that manifests itself in materialism, externalism, comparison, competition, revenge, envy, covetousness, fear, and anger.

Jesus said that we must become like a child in order to become a part of the kingdom (Luke 18:17). That's a tough call for most, who spend vast amounts of time and energy on being perceived as anything but childish. Our education, sophistication, seasoning, and reasoning take us away from this call. Yet unless we understand the paradox, we'll miss the point. On one side of the SI continuum there's a mind set we'll call *childish*. Here we see immature qualities such as naivete, temper tantrums, failure to share, self-centeredness, whining, and complaining. But on the other side is a mind set we'll call *childlike*. This is characterized with innocence, trust, love, laughter, simplicity, and curiosity. God calls us to the latter.

Low SI/Shallow	Medium SI	High SI/Deep
Immature/Simplicity	Mixed/Complex	Mature/Simplicity

Both mind sets, childishness and childlikeness, are marked by simplicity. As Buchanan said, "There is a simplicity that exists on the far side of complexity, and there is a communication of sentiment and attitude not to be discovered by careful exegesis of a text." Most adults get caught up in complexity issues so that they are unaware of anything else, or they become so jaded that they move back toward immature simplicity. On the other side of complexity exists a quality of life that is very parklike in nature, a place that resonates with peace, love, joy, and other spiritual fruit, ripe for the picking. SI takes us there.

Your One Thing

"'My food,' said Jesus, 'is to do the will of him who sent me and to finish his work'" (John 4:34). "For I have come down from heaven not to do my will but to do the will of him who sent me" (John 6:38).

To legitimately live striving to do God's will is a freedom rarely experienced. People establish fiscal, physical, mental, and work goals, often with little pursuit of divine wisdom. Achieved or not, these goals become badges of honor, elevating our perceived value to the world. "Look at my noble, lofty pursuits. Check out the hood ornament on my car, the framed certificates on my office walls, and the square footage of my house. My life has meaning."

When I was young, people asked, "What do you want to achieve in life?" I used to have a list of four priorities: pastor a dynamic church, write, speak, and develop a leadership center. My wife would then remind me that my kids and family should be a priority as well, so I'd oblige her by saying, "Well, of course, that's a given." I had a mental image of the house, books, church building, and life I would someday obtain, "out of service for Christ," naturally. I meant it. My motive was to accomplish these things because I believed God had put them in me to birth. But ultimately these pursuits were self-serving.

The spiritually intelligent answer to the question "What do you want to achieve in life?" is this: "To do God's will." A response like that simplifies life. It also requires that I seek

God and submit to his will once I find it. God gives us enough time every day to do his will. When I am rushed and frantic, it's a sign that I've either squandered my time, am pursuing things not in his plan, or both. While I still have goals, they are not measured by my previous standards. I may accomplish many of them, but they are by-products, like so much scenery out the car window along my trek.

Wishes abound. Dreams persist. But more and more, my pursuit is to listen to and please my Maker. Life is short. Eternity is long. I'm called to respond to the divine call, not to accomplish everything I'm able. America has developed an entrepreneurial faith, striving for bigger and better accomplishments in the name of Jesus. We buy into the idea that if God is in it, it should be growing, slick, and giant. This path leads to unhealthy patterns such as pride, incessant discontentment, envy, and discouragement. Those in professional ministry know that discouragement is their greatest foe. We've created a mutant form of spirituality that drives us to many kinds of neurotic thoughts. One goes like this: "Instead of merely accomplishing God's will, it's my job to do all I can to further the cause of Christ, to work smarter, harder, and faster so I can accomplish more, more, and more." Imagine the simplicity of facing each day with a simple goal: "God, what do you want me to do? What is your will?"

5-D (Life in the Fifth Dimension)

How do you maintain this perspective? How do you live out the sort of commitment required for soul growth? Spiritual ends require spiritual means. As humans, with tangible bodies, much of our lives are consumed three-dimensionally. The 3-D realm is where we negotiate our lives for the purpose of staying alive, going places, and working. I define the fourth dimension as the realm of emotional and mental energy. We relate to people in this arena in ways that transcend the first three dimensions. This dimension is intangible, but often results in tangible expressions, such as solving problems, writing love notes, and speaking our feelings.

But one more dimension exists that people rarely acknowledge in terms of daily, practical applications. This is the fifth dimension, the realm of the spiritual, supernatural, and divine. Greek mythology writers conjured up all sorts of theories about life among the gods, and contemporary society is expressing renewed interest in the supernatural. Belief in the spiritual dimension appeared to be ebbing during modernity, when people began assuming everything could be explained through a scientific formula and laboratory investigation. But science was found wanting. People everywhere seem to know in their bones there is more to life.

But when people can't locate that something more, they tend to fill this sacred space with substitutes, often demeaning those who claim to find it in God. This should not intimidate us. "The man without the Spirit does not accept the things that come from the Spirit of God, for they are foolishness to him, and he cannot understand them, because they are spiritually discerned" (1 Cor. 2:14).

The spiritual should not be taken lightly. It is just as real as the book you hold, the car you drive, and the food you eat. Navigating the fifth dimension requires discipline and discernment. "Dear friends, do not believe every spirit, but test the spirits to see whether they are from God, because many false prophets have gone out into the world" (1 John 4:1).

While fifth-dimension living as we know it does not take us out of the first four, it certainly impacts them. The person who has committed himself or herself to the pursuit of this dimension is apt to experience numerous new ideas, perspectives, and emerging behaviors. Fifth-dimension living is what the Bible refers to as life in the Spirit, but Spirit-filled living as is commonly described in church circles often does not adequately reflect fifth-dimension living.

Just as a pilot learns to fly by instrument flight rules, we must acquire the same skills spiritually, not relying solely on what is visible. "Now it is God who has made us for this very purpose and has given us the Spirit as a deposit, guaranteeing what is to come. . . . Live by faith, not by sight" (2 Cor. 5:5, 7). Most never make it this far, stopping at the threshold of the fifth dimension, setting up camp outside its gates, settling in a comfort zone of presence minus power. Fifth-dimension living is not only what SI leads to, it is the lifestyle required for spiritual path walking. You'll only get so far down the road unless you begin to intentionally pursue life in the fifth dimension. Spiritual intelligence allows you to be fully engaged in all five dimensions.

A Closing Blessing

I want to say thanks for taking this journey with me to discover how it is that Jesus grew the souls of those around him, in hopes that we too might experience the type of results that rocked the world. This closing blessing is based on Psalm 84.

> My soul yearns, even faints,
> for the courts of the LORD;
> my heart and my flesh cry out
> for the living God.

This is the DNA of spiritual intelligence: a soul that yearns for the presence of God, in spite of circumstances, emotions, and externals.

> Blessed are those whose strength is in you,
> who have set their hearts on pilgrimage.

SI is about pilgrimage, a journey motivated by our design, toward fulfilling our purpose. May you set your heart on this quest.

They go from strength to strength,
till each appears before God in Zion.

SI involves ever growing, never giving up, even when you feel like it. May you move from strength to strength in spite of weak times and valleys.

Better is one day in your courts
than a thousand elsewhere;
I would rather be a doorkeeper in the house of my
God
than dwell in the tents of the wicked.

SI allows you to discover that there are far greater things in life than acquisition and human success. May God show you this type of achievement.

For the LORD God is a sun and shield;
the LORD bestows favor and honor;
no good thing does he withhold
from those whose walk is blameless.

SI is not about status quo, but acquiring more of the right thing. May God show you favor and honor in your work, your relationships, and your being.

O LORD Almighty,
blessed is the [person] who trusts in you.

The outcome of spiritual intelligence is an abundant life. May you obtain life's ultimate goal, God's blessing.

Psalm 84:2, 5, 7, 10–12

The Journey

A Spiritual Health Assessment and Development Plan

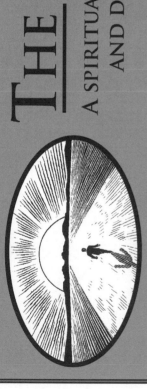

THE JOURNEY:

A SPIRITUAL HEALTH ASSESSMENT
AND DEVELOPMENT PLAN

Name _____ Date _____ Age/Gender _____ / _____

Street Address/City/State/Zip/Contact Info: _____

_____

NARRATIVE SNAPSHOT: *(Respond to the following issues as succinctly as possible.)*

Write a brief spiritual (church/religious) history of your life:

_____

_____

_____

_____

_____

_____

List your perceived strengths/gifts and serving experiences:

_____

_____

_____

Spiritual/religious education/learning (who, what, when, where, how):

_____

_____

_____

How would you describe your spiritual health the last six months?

_____

_____

_____

1

LIFELINE Instructions:

1. Write 8-12 significant events of your life in chronological order, top to bottom.
2. On the graph below, list your birth year and today's date.
3. The asterisk represents your birth, so place numbered dots from left to right, corresponding with the significant events, above or below the midline, depending on whether they were positive or negative, respectively.
4. Connect the dots to plot a simple line graph. You may have two lines at times, if for example, a negative life event was at the same time making a positive spiritual impact.

SIGNIFICANT LIFE EVENTS/TIMES

1. _____

2. _____

3. _____

4. _____

5. _____

6. _____

7. _____

8. _____

9. _____

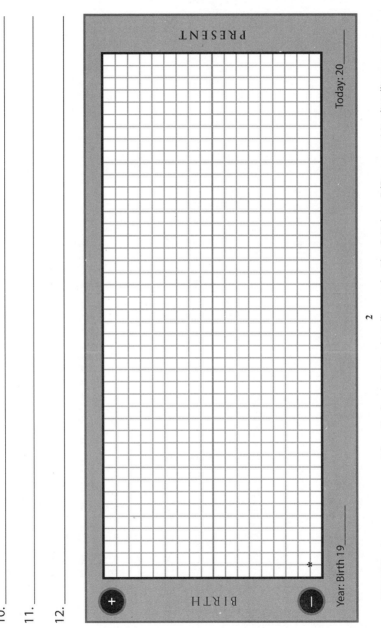

10. _____

11. _____

12. _____

PRESENT

BIRTH

+

–

Year: Birth 19_____

Today: 20_____

©2009 The Journey assessment from the book: Spiritual Intelligence by Alan E. Nelson, EdD, www.spiritualintelligance.org

GROWTH INDICATOR: (*Instructions: Answer the following 20 questions with answers 1-5: 1-rarely to nonexistent, 2-little, 3-off and on, 4-quite a bit, 5-consistently and with excellence*).

(Items 1-9: Fruit(s) of the Spirit; Gal. 5:22-23)

___ 1. Loving: I am accepting and gracious, non-critical or judgmental toward other people in what I say and how I interact with them.

___ 2. Joyful: I exude a positive, hopeful, optimistic attitude.

___ 3. Peaceful: I display inner tranquility and harmony, in spite of circumstances; content.

___ 4. Patience: I suffer long under slow and/or adverse conditions; not easily angered or irritable.

___ 5. Kind: I am respectful, friendly, and complimentary in my relationships.

___ 6. Goodness: I stand up for what is right and avoid moral compromise.

___ 7. Faithful: I am consistent in my devotion to and trust of God.

___ 8. Gentle: I am easy to be around and sensitive to the feelings of others.

___ 9. Self-Control/Self-Discipline: I am able to deny my urges and put off self-gratification.

___ 10. Witnessing: I share my faith verbally and/or invite people to church. (Matthew 5:16)

___ 11. Time Stewardship: I use my time well, both working hard as well as investing in Sabbath for worship and relaxation. (James 4:14-15)

_____ 12. Connection (community, accountability, care): I am involved in an active small group, designed around prayer, study, friendship and accountability. (Hebrews 10:25)

_____ 13. Biblical Knowledge/Doctrine: I am actively involved in studying the Bible and stretching myself mentally to learn more. (Hebrews 4:12)

_____ 14. Service Involvement: I am aware of my ministry gifts and am involved in an ongoing role, using them to serve others. (1 Corinthians 12:27)

_____ 15. Humility: I demonstrate humility (admit wrong, ask for help, avoid defensiveness, don't brag, and serve anonymously). (Proverbs 18:12)

_____ 16. Forgiveness/Grace Sharing: I forgive quickly and avoid holding grudges. (Matthew 18:21-22)

_____ 17. Others Focus (vs. self): I put the needs of others first on a consistent basis and voluntarily, with a positive attitude. (Philippians 2:3)

_____ 18. Money: I regularly commit significant amounts of my funds to the needy and/or God's work. (Malachi 3:7-8)

_____ 19. Time Alone With God/Prayer: I consistently invest quality time, alone with God for Bible study, spiritual reading, prayer, and meditation. (Matthew 6:6)

_____ 20. Worldview/Mission-Minded: I carry an ongoing burden for people in other cultures to grow spiritually, pray for them, and give time/money to missions. (Mark 16:15)

3

Progress Plotter: *(We express our spiritual growth in four primary arenas. Rate yourself on a 1-5 scale in each of these areas, per the defined levels.)*

	Knowledge: Awareness of Bible content, doctrine, and knowing how to study Scriptures and discern God's truth.	**Attitudes:** How we handle our emotions and responses to circumstances.	**Behavior:** The way we act in terms of moral & lifestyle issues; deeds, works.	**Relationships:** The quality of our social interactions; love, peace, forgiveness, giving grace, and serving others.
Level 5: Pouring yourself into others so that they mature because of your influence.				
Level 4: Strong on your own; able to respond well as issues arise in this area.				
Level 3: Generally stable in this area; showing growth but noted areas for improvement.				
Level 2: Up and down; unsure where you'll be from day to day; generally unstable.				
Level 1: Struggling; some major challenges in this area that are negatively affecting your soul.				

Next Steps: *(Prayerfully and possibly with the help of a Path Finder or spiritually mature assistant, write out a realistic plan for spiritual growth, which might include specific events, programs, weekly disciplines, study areas, and/or accountability relationships which will make this realistic. Review the plan regularly and re-take The Journey in 6-18 months.)*

Path Finder/mentor's name: _____

What were your lower Spiritual Intelligence Plotter cell(s) and 3-5 lowest Soul Growth Indicator items that showed up in your self-evaluation or feedback from others?

Teaching: What do you need to study in the coming weeks/months to address these issues? How will you obtain adequate teaching in these areas?

Accountability: What small group or individual can you make a covenant with to hold you accountable for growth in these specific areas? How will you establish accountability?

Mentor/model: Who can you establish a mentoring relationship with who might help you grow in these specific areas? Who can you mentor in order to help them grow as well as stretching yourself?

Experience: What experiential events or commitments can you develop that will help you to grow in these areas? List times, events, deadlines, and other details:

4

©2009 The Journey assessment from the book: Spiritual Intelligence by Alan E. Nelson, EdD, www.spiritualintelligance.org

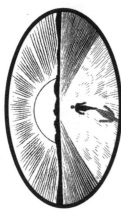

Next Step Soul Growth Suggestions for

Path Finder _____ Date _____

Target #1: _____

Strategy: _____

_____

_____

Target #2: _____

Strategy: _____

_____

_____

Target #3: _____

Strategy: _____

_____

_____

Target #4: _____

Strategy: _____

_____

_____

Hi! Would you please answer these questions with (*name*) _____
in mind, for a personal growth survey? This assessment looks at a variety of aspects, related to both behaviors and attitudes. Your answers will be confidential and your feedback is appreciated. Please respond if possible within 1 week. (Target date needed: ___/___/___)

Instructions: To the best of your ability, answer the following questions on a 1-5 scale: 1-rarely to nonexistent, 2-little, 3-off and on, 4-quite a bit, 5-consistently and with excellence.

____ 1. Honoring: This person is honoring, gracious, accepting and non-judgmental toward other people in what s/he says and how s/he interacts with them.

____ 2. Joyful: This person exudes a positive, hopeful, optimistic attitude.

____ 3. Peaceful: This person displays inner tranquility and harmony, in spite of circumstances; seems content.

____ 4. Patience: This person suffers long under slow and/or adverse conditions; not easily angered or irritable.

____ 5. Kind: This person is respectful, friendly, and complimentary in his/her relationships.

____ 6. Ethical: This person stands up for what is right and avoids moral compromise; has integrity; does what s/he says s/he'll do.

____ 7. Faithful: This person seems to exude a strong faith in God.

____ 8. Gentle: This person is easy to be around and sensitive to the feelings of others.

_____ 9. Self-control: This person is self disciplined, able to deny his/her urges and delay gratification.

_____ 10. Spiritual: This person is comfortable talking about his/her faith without offending or being offended.

_____ 11. Time Use: This person seems to use time well, working hard, but also taking time to rest, spend time with friends and spiritual renewal.

_____ 12. Connection: Is involved with a small group, designed around encouragement, accountability, and spiritual growth.

_____ 13. Bible knowledge: Is actively involved in reading and studying the Bible.

_____ 14. Service involvement: Is active in serving others without pay; servant attitude.

_____ 15. Humility: Admits wrong, asks for help, avoids defensiveness, doesn't brag.

_____ 16. Forgiveness: Forgives quickly and avoids holding grudges; is gracious.

_____ 17. Others focus: Puts the needs of others first on a consistent basis; not self-centered.

_____ 18. This person is generous financially to help the needy and support charities.

_____ 19. This person takes time for prayer, meditation, and seeks Divine wisdom in big decisions.

_____ 20. This person expresses interest and concern for people in other cultures.

©2009 The Journey assessment from the book: Spiritual Intelligence by Alan E. Nelson, EdD, www.spiritualintelligance.org

The SI Church

Traditional methods used by churches will typically result in spiritual growth, but rarely maturity. A growing number of honest, committed leaders are recognizing this trend. As demonstrated in George Barna's research with those he calls "Revolutionaries," Alan Jamieson's studies reported in *The Churchless Faith*, and Willow Creek's "Reveal" surveys, more of us in church life are getting real with the results. I am interacting with a growing number of spiritually astute people who are confidentially sharing their frustration in finding a congregation that challenges them personally.

As a longtime pastor and one who continues to work with scores of pastors around the country, I deeply respect most church leaders. But the typical church will not be able to produce people with SI as it hopes, so long as it continues traditional means and fails to implement Jesus's method of soul growth. No amount of preaching about Jesus or explaining his teaching will produce the same results as Jesus's methods. The mantra of pastors must become "DWJD": Do What Jesus Did.

Most congregations can make significant improvement by helping people develop their own soul growth plans, so long as they align with the methods Jesus used. While communicating the need for each person to take his or her own responsibility in soul growth, pastors and congregations can make significant steps toward helping people obtain SI. Here are some ideas on what will likely need to happen in the typical church for it to develop SI in its congregation.

1. *The pastor needs to lead the effort.* This is true of nearly any change initiative, if there is a chance for implementation. Rarely can a church experience a significant transition without the pastor championing the idea. That often requires the pastor to modify his or her identity, because much of what pastors do is wrapped up in who they perceive they are in their role. The typical identity is based around conducting traditional church services, no matter how contemporary, cool, or edgy they are, consisting of sermons, group singing, and programmatic ministries. While these can be employed by people using SI methods, they are not in and of themselves sufficient to produce the sort of growth we desire in our people. Therefore, pastors need to embrace the idea for change and begin rethinking what it is the church should invest in and provide for its people. Dr. Phil is famous for asking, "Is it working for you?" As long as you think what you're doing works, there's little chance that you'll pay the price for change.

One of the most provocative things you can do is to read this book as a group of leaders and discuss what you presently provide, in the context of what Jesus did with his learners. This honest-to-God conversation is apt to raise both concerns and some temperatures. Most ministry leaders are heavily invested in doing what they do, but the discussion will do you good to begin rethinking why you do what you do and how effective you really are in producing people with SI. Discussions like this can lead to vision casting for different and more effective methods of soul growth.

2. *The pastor must transition from expert to coach.* Pastors are tellers by nature. We are answer people, whom con-

gregants seek for Bible knowledge, discernment in hearing God's voice, and overall spiritual guidance. But in the new paradigm, the pastor is far more coach than commander. Your responsibility is not so much to provide answers as it is to catalyze new thinking. The goal is empowerment. If you create a relationship where people are dependent on you, they will rarely take responsibility for their own soul growth. None of us have the time or resources to provide customized, hand-holding guidance for each person under our care. Rather, we want to create an atmosphere where people are challenged to think for themselves and own the solution. This is not to imply that you never provide solutions, but your goal is to brainstorm options, along with potential costs and benefits, far more than selling solutions. Grow thinkers, not robots.

3. *Facilitate the creation and nurturing of Travel Teams.* What you call these groups in your ministry context is immaterial, so long as they aren't encumbered with baggage from the past. Words are powerful, so avoid recycling existing or old names in hopes of sneaking in new methods under the radar. Obviously, Jesus did not refer to his disciples as a Travel Team. This is part of an overarching metaphor in this book. Make it your own. Just be cautious to keep the methods true to their original design and not dilute them to fit your current structure, which is likely imported from traditions, historical or contemporary.

What are you currently doing that truly reflects the methods Jesus used, instead of what is traditionally a church event or program? I've heard of churches that have literally stopped everything other than their Sunday morning worship service, in order to retool according to different values. If you are beginning a new church from scratch, you may want to rethink everything you do from the start. How can you make Jesus's methods core to all you do, not just ancillary or à la carte menu options? So long as it's seen as a nonessential program, it will become a ministry island like any other program.

If you want to launch significantly, begin with one or two "turbo groups." A turbo group consists of a Travel Team whose members are invited with the intent of becoming Path Finders for other Travel Teams. That is what Jesus did, ordaining the Twelve to go into the world and make other learners. Be honest about your intent at the start, so that people are aware of why it is they were selected and what it is you expect from them at the end. After nine months, you may be able to unleash these individuals with teams of their own, even while they continue in their original team. This way, you can continue to coach these people as they run into their own challenges.

4. *Use weekend worship services as feeder pools for Travel Teams.* While shrinking, there is still a significant segment in society more apt to show up for a regular weekend worship service than align with a Travel Team. In an SI church, the pastor will continually remind congregants that the engine driving the church is the Travel Teams. "Our goal is to help you develop your own soul growth plan." Preach it, teach it, and talk about it, so that it becomes a part of the fabric of your congregation. Weekend services provide places for people to become comfortable with your church in general, but their greatest growth is most likely to take place in the context of a Travel Team.

5. *Make the Travel Teams a part of your continual church life and communication.* Mention them in your messages. Talk about them before and after church, in newsletters, announcements, and testimonials of people. This is not a program, even though you're helping facilitate these relationships. The goal is to create an atmosphere where people feel a yearning to get more involved and participate in a more effective means of soul growth. Analyze everything your church does in the context of supporting or promoting Jesus's methods relating to SI.

An example of what this might look like in terms of a Sunday morning worship service bulletin announcement is as follows: "Those of you using today's message for your Directions may find the following questions helpful as you discuss this in your Travel Team meeting this week." If you're promoting a community service project, you could suggest that "Path Finders may want to consider the upcoming workday at the homeless shelter as an Experiencing the Trip opportunity."

The idea is to add simple labels and instructions to what you're already providing, to show how to implement these for congregants using the SI methods.

6. *Tell stories in messages and highlight Travel Teams.* Jesus frequently used the power of story. The Bible is a veritable compilation of stories, depicting how people interact with God. Gathering these and then processing them for newsletters, websites, sermon illustrations, video testimonials, and live storytelling are important means of communicating these values. You may begin to think of your large group gatherings as a means for story sharing. The organized church can serve as a vehicle for harvesting and communicating themes of people experiencing life transformation and serving others. Doing this creatively is important for maintaining interest in a media-cultured society. Implementing the arts is a wonderful means of this as well.

7. *Encourage weekend activities that focus on Travel Teams.* Many churches frown on small groups or ministries scheduling retreats or events over weekends, because it reduces attendance and depletes available volunteers. But when your emphasis is on Experiencing the Trip and providing opportunities for Travel Teams to interact outside of passive study settings, you'll fan the flames for people getting away together when they're able around work schedules. If traditionalists are concerned about attendance or offering, then figure out how to include the people in your total and perhaps even find a means for them to turn in their offerings before, during, or after the getaway. Chances are that these people will grow

more spiritually by serving together and investing a large chunk of time away than they will by attending a one- or two-hour worship service. Suggest, promote, encourage, and defend this practice. Consider canceling weekend services from time to time to highlight serving others. Let the Travel Teams organize the entire congregation for community involvement. This is but one way of conveying the message that you're far more about action and service than passivity and intellectualism.

8. *Create a "People Development" plan for your church.* Make this a very intentional written document, showing how your congregation plans to help people achieve their spiritual goals. Hardly any church has a document like this. The closest thing tends to be a mission statement, set of doctrinal beliefs, and a brochure or two on how to become a member and a list of various ministries and events. How do you teach people about growing their souls through your church? While a four-point ball diamond is a good start, what is a more organic process that helps people see where they can go and how you intend to assist them in their journey? Then provide a graphic or schematic presentation to visually communicate the process and make it readily available, then refer to it frequently. Begin with the type of people you want to produce and then work backward, including measuring tools, connecting points, communication channels, and contact information.

9. *Screen, gather, and make available recommended "Directions" resources.* You don't have to toss your unique tribal doctrines and theology out the window just because you're using Jesus's methods, but one service you provide as a church may be a gathering and screening process. This makes it easy for Path Finders who are looking for grounded resources. Don't limit these to a short list of books or formal Bible studies. Consider other teaching resources, people, and media. Better yet, train Path Finders in how to find their own re-

sources, empowering them to do this responsibly. The role of staff becomes one of equipping, not just "doing" ministry. The result is ministry multiplication.

10. *Provide a coaching network among your Path Finders.* You'll want to provide ongoing coaching and quality assessment for Path Finder accountability and improvement. You can do this through weekly, biweekly, monthly, or quarterly meetings that include discussion, training, feedback, and mentoring. Even though you're creating a decentralized ministry structure, you can continue to develop the influencers, monitor progress, communicate vision, and gather feedback for developing effective support resources for the Travel Teams. I am not advocating anything specifically because it will likely look different in your church. Just as Moses had some sort of development system that he used to empower scores of people who provided care for an entire nation (Exodus 18), you'll need to come up with a communication and leadership development process. The church's greatest value is to develop people, not recruiting people to develop the church. When this happens, you'll have a congregation cultivating SI among those in its reach.

Church Change

Years ago, I wrote a book with a friend of mine, called *How to Change Your Church*. Over time, I've had the opportunity to train and consult many pastors and leaders in how to effectively implement improvement ideas in ways that won't harm them or set them back as a result. A wise congregational leader needs to be very savvy in how he or she goes about transitioning a congregation. Most will likely find significant resistance to implementing these ideas, even though they are ones that Jesus utilized. The reason is that organizations have the inherent DNA to perpetuate themselves. The natural result is a somewhat automatic rejection of ideas that are not within the existing comfort zone. You'll do best to make a list of the influencers in your church, formal or informal, and then figure out who tends to be more receptive to new ideas and who is less responsive.

Gather your more receptive influencers to form a discussion group, to read and dialogue about the concepts in this book. Let the participants know that you're thinking about new ways of doing ministry in order to improve how your church helps people grow spiritually. Chances are you'll find a receptive attitude among these people, because most people eventually see the gap between SI and existing church involvement. Only after these people have bought into the idea will you want to expand the dream to others. Creating a critical mass behind a new idea is essential if the new idea has a chance of surviving. Then gradually roll it out without a lot of fanfare or hoopla. Quietly begin implementing some of the methods we've discussed. After several months or even a year or two, let the grapevine begin to pique curiosity. Allow stories to percolate, and harvest them.

See this as a slow on-ramp more than an abrupt loading dock. As you gradually move toward Jesus's method of growing souls and the church serving as a means for this, then you'll be able to begin making more dramatic changes in terms of staffing, scheduling, programming, and resources. After a while, your congregation will probably look quite different than most, but you'll be seeing significant growth and maturity with far less time and energy in buildings and programs. The church will become a resource and coaching center, more than a place to go for religious programs and events.